A
GRE
ANTHOLO

N° 2512

THE HULTON DEUTSCH COLLECTION

A
GRESLEY
ANTHOLOGY
EDITED BY GEOFFREY HUGHES

HERBERT NIGEL GRESLEY c.1933.

Half a century of locomotive development is illustrated by this 1922 photograph of Patrick Stirling's No. 1, and H. N. Gresley's new Pacific, GNR No. 1471.
EDITOR'S COLLECTION

INTRODUCTION

A Gresley Anthology is a selection of articles written over a period of twenty years for *The Gresley Observer*, the Journal of the Gresley Society. The authors are varied, but all are experts in their knowledge of Sir Nigel Gresley's locomotives and trains. J. F. Harrison and Terry Miller were Doncaster apprentices who went on to occupy the post of Chief Mechanical Engineer of British Railways. Gerard Fiennes was an LNER traffic apprentice who ended his career as a General Manager; Norman Newsome was one of Sir Nigel's technical assistants. Arthur Taylor, Charlie Peachey, Bert Collins and F. G. Fowler speak from the footplate, and Bill Harvey and Sid Checkley discuss the problems of locomotive maintenance. Michael Joyce, Eric Neve, John Clay and David Lowther are distinguished observers of the LNER scene. Further, most of the illustrations are from photographs taken by members of the Gresley Society.

The memory of Sir Nigel Gresley is kept alive by the rich fund of material which continues to appear in *The Gresley Observer*, and readers who would like to find out more about the Gresley Society are invited to write to the Hon. Secretary, G. W. Goslin, 8 Pevensey Grove, Flitwick, Bedford, MK45 1SD.

We are grateful to Paul Karau and Wild Swan Publications Ltd for the initiative which has resulted in the publication of this book, and hope that it will give information and pleasure to all who are interested in the steam locomotive, particularly those who enjoy reading about the sight and sound of Gresley locomotives, on the road and in the workshops.

Dr. Geoffrey Hughes
Hon Editor
The Gresley Observer

CONTENTS

ISBN 1 874103 19 4

Designed by Paul Karau
Printed by Amadeus Press Ltd., Huddersfield

Published by

WILD SWAN PUBLICATIONS LTD.
1-3 Hagbourne Road, Didcot, Oxon, OX11 8DP

Cover photo: Silver Link at King's Cross in September 1935. The original recessed draw hook shows up well in this picture, the streamlined casing protruding about 1ft in front of the buffer beam. The first four engines were built like this, but after a fatal accident at King's Cross due to limited clearance buffering-up to stock, a longer draw hook and buffers were fitted to all later engines. The first four were also subsequently modified.
THE HULTON DEUTSCH COLLECTION

No. 2750 Papyrus leaving King's Cross at the start of a record-breaking run to Newcastle and back to test the practicality of running the high-speed trains. Many records were broken on this run, one, the 108 mph achieved on the return journey, breaking the world record for steam.
THE HULTON DEUTSCH COLLECTION

THE STREAMLINE TRAINS
MEMORIES OF THE GRESLEY STREAMLINERS

ERIC NEVE

Judging by the number of spectators, this is probably the initial departure of the 'Silver Jubilee' from King's Cross. The locomotive is Silver Link.
H. N. JAMES

AFTER the London–Leeds return test run on 30th November 1934 using A1 No 4472 *Flying Scotsman* and then A3 2750 *Papyrus* to Newcastle and back on 5th March 1935, during which maximum speeds of 100 and 108 mph respectively were attained, all Gresley supporters in the Northern Heights were prepared for the new improved Pacific for use on the projected 'Silver Jubilee' express to commence in September 1935. None, however, was fully prepared for the revolutionary streamlined exterior of both locomotive and train in silver grey livery.

As one who did have the satisfaction of watching the first public journey by the new A4 No 2509 *Silver Link* with the 7.10 am from King's Cross to Cambridge on 14th September, it is a sobering thought that this was 50 years ago. It was a lovely sunny morning as the eagerly awaited new engine came into view running gently and quietly on the down slow line. The outline

was a shock to one brought up to admire the graceful lines of Ivatt Atlantics and the Gresley A1 and A3 Pacifics. On return to King's Cross at 1.37 pm, 2509 went on to Top Shed where it was photographed for the *Railway Gazette* and by members of the Stephenson Locomotive Society who had an official visit that day.

A second trip was made to Cambridge on Monday, 16th September, and then on the Wednesday and Thursday a double trip to Peterborough took place on the 7.45 am slow, returning at 11.38 am with the combined Leeds and Cleethorpes express due into King's Cross at 1.3 pm. After a short rest, 2509 went to Grantham and back on the 5.45 pm Hull express, returning thence at 9.5 pm with a braked meat (10.45 am ex Aberdeen) due into East Goods at 11.20 pm. No record is shown in London observers' notebooks for 20th–22nd September. According to *Gresley Observer* No 56, September 1975, page 71, the engine worked a special brake

trial from Doncaster to Peterborough and back on the 20th, but it is stated in the RCTS *Locomotives of the LNER* Part 2A, page 122, that this took place on 22nd September. (Which is correct?) Inexplicably, on Monday the 23rd *Silver Link* went only to Grantham on the 1.20 pm Edinburgh express from King's Cross, normally a through working to Newcastle, and was not seen again until Thursday the 26th, on the 4.15 pm semi-fast to Peterborough, returning on the heavy 5.30 pm ex Leeds leaving Peterborough at 8.0 pm, due King's Cross at 9.25 pm. After the historic trial trip to Barkston and back on Friday the 27th, on the following day *Silver Link* made two return trips to Peterborough on the 7.45 am (Driver Taylor) and 4.15 pm (Driver Sparshatt).

Vivid memories remain of the keen sense of anticipation at King's Cross as we awaited the return of the trial run on Friday, 27th September 1935. Nothing was known in advance of what had occurred

1

No. 2510 Quicksilver *heading south through Sandy on 1st May 1937.*

L. HANSON

nor had most of us seen the new train set. As the train came gently to a stand in Platform 4, Mr Gresley (as he then was), hatless and obviously excited, descended from the footplate, flourishing his 'chronograph of vast dimensions', as Cecil J. Allen described it, and exclaiming to waiting newsmen '112 miles an hour, 112 miles an hour!' The excitement having died down, the ordinary observers were able to walk along the platform admiring the new train, featuring standards hitherto undreamed of. As we walked back, the 3.30 pm from Peterborough 'Parly' ran into Platform 2 headed by a graceful Ivatt 'Klondyke' (one of the first British Atlantics, dating from 1898). It came to a stand opposite the new streamlined Pacific and, as we stopped to admire the little 'Klondyke' we had no doubts at that moment as to which outline we preferred.

It has been said that the introduction of the high speed schedule into the Working Time Table caused havoc to other trains. However, this is not borne out insofar as the GN main line is concerned. For the 5.30 pm departure, the 5.10 pm to Baldock had to be turned slow line at Woolmer Green and the 5.0 pm to Peterborough from Sandy to St Neot's,

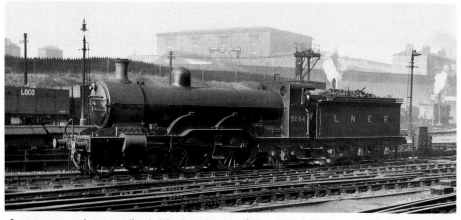

In contrast to the streamlined A4s, here is one of the original 'Klondykes', No. 3254, at Top Shed, King's Cross, in the 1930s.

S. FREESE

making it nine minutes later into Peterborough. Coming up, the 11.25 am Doncaster–Peterborough slow had to wait 10 minutes at Retford, and the 1.15 Hitchin–King's Cross 11 minutes at Knebworth. It was only from 1937 when the 'Coronation' and 'West Riding Limited' were put on that rather more complications arose.

The King's Cross Top Shed No 1 'Newcastle Lodge' link, which had comprised six sets of enginemen for at least eight years, was increased to eight sets in September

1935 to cover the extra two sets weekly required to operate the 'Silver Jubilee'. The longest serving driver was H. Gutteridge who had been in the link from May 1928. Next came W. Sparshatt (July 1931); A. Taylor (April 1932); W. Samwells (December 1932); W. Payne (December 1933) and C. Peachey (April 1934). Of these six drivers only Sparshatt and Payne had seen service in the No 1A 'Leeds Pullman' link which had provided opportunity for some fast running over the years, with Atlantics. The two additional drivers were G. Burfoot and G. Haygreen promoted from No 2 link in which they had led rather a sheltered existence as the nine-week roster included three weeks each to Grantham and Cambridge and three complete weeks on each of the three King's Cross Main Line Pilot duties. In the summer seasons 1934–35 both had elected to take the rather 'cushy' job on the non-stop 'Flying Scotsman', on which they worked the Haymarket Pacific from London to Tollerton and then travelled on the cushions and obtained a nice free lunch en route to Edinburgh. Next day they travelled in the train to Tollerton and worked to King's Cross. They alternated on this duty, usually making one return trip to Edinburgh followed by two days on the 10.50 am King's Cross–Peterborough slow and 2.48 pm return with the express due King's Cross at 4.15 pm. Although their seniority would have allowed them to go into No 1 link in 1933, rather than Messrs Payne and Peachey, they decided to remain in No 2 until the chance of some glory working the streamlined train arose in 1935. Burfoot made a success of his

No. 2512 Silver Fox, *ex-works at Doncaster in December 1935. This loco was in regular use on the 'Silver Jubilee', and remained at King's Cross shed until almost the end of its working life.* LNER

The stainless steel emblem of a silver fox, affixed to No. 2512 from new, provided by the steelmakers Samuel Fox & Co.
H. N. JAMES

Five of the A4s were named after Commonwealth countries, and were provided with the appropriate coat-of-arms. No. 4489 is Dominion of Canada.
H. N. JAMES

sojourn in No I link, but Haygreen decided to retire early in September 1936 soon after his unfortunate run with *Silver Fox* on the dynamometer car test.

It is worth repeating that as the second A4, 2510 *Quicksilver*, was not ready to undertake high speed work until Thursday, 17th October, *Silver Link* worked the 'Silver Jubilee' express on 23 occasions in each direction. No 2510 then made only one return trip, down on 17th and up next day, and then 2509 went down on the 18th again.

Thus in the autumn of 1935 it could be justly claimed that Gresley and his team, aided by the traditional craftsmanship of Doncaster workmen, brought the dawn of a new era in British locomotive history. The A4 Pacifics were indeed 'Machines of supreme competence', as one contemporary writer put it. The faith of the Northern Heights supporters was amply justified for at last the 'opposition' from those favouring the GWR and the so-called 'Premier Line' was silenced.

In contrast to the 'Silver Jubilee', three sheds took part in the working of the 'Coronation'. King's Cross and Haymarket supplied both engines and men, but Gateshead provided men only. At first, when the train stopped only at York going down, crews were changed there, the King's Cross men handing over to Haymarket men and the Gateshead men to another crew from their home shed. When the Newcastle stop was inserted, crews from King's Cross and Gateshead worked to Newcastle, there handing over to Haymarket men who had worked the up train from Edinburgh. On Sundays King's Cross engine and men went down on the 1.0 pm express, the men changing at Newcastle and the engine working through to Edinburgh. The Haymarket engine left Edinburgh at 11.40 am for Newcastle, where it came off and waited

No. 2511 Silver King *was the reserve engine for the 'Silver Jubilee'. Stationed at Gateshead, it was not often seen in London, but here it is passing Ferme Park with the up train. The Hornsey loco coaling plant can be seen in the background.*
COLLECTION A. B. COLLINS

Silver Fox *at Newcastle Central station. In addition to the fox, the casing was also adorned with stainless steel boiler lagging bands. There was a proposal to fit complete stainless steel boiler cladding plates, but this did not come to fruition.*
EDITOR'S COLLECTION

No. 4498 Sir Nigel Gresley *approaching Potters Bar with the down 'Coronation'. The location has now completely changed, with the widening to four lines and the rebuilding of the station.*   GRESLEY SOCIETY COLLECTION

The 'Coronation' passing Ranskill, featuring the beaver tail observation coach. Two of these were provided during the summer months, one for each train, numbered 1719 and (this one) 1729.   C. L. TURNER

As well as heading the initial down working, No. 4491 Commonwealth of Australia was one of the most regular performers on the 'Coronation'. It is seen here on the up train near Cockburnspath.
C. L. TURNER

until 5.20 pm to work through to London with a Gateshead crew. This method meant that both engines returned to their home shed on Fridays, thus eliminating any Saturday turns. So Gateshead worked the 4.0 pm down on Mondays, Wednesdays and Fridays and King's Cross on Tuesdays and Thursdays.

On an unrecorded date in December 1937, No 4490 was removed from the up 'Coronation' at Hatfield, leaving N1 No 4582 to work on to King's Cross. On 4th January 1939, No 4482 failed at Grantham on the down train and was replaced by W1 No 10000, which also failed at Durham, where G5 No 1837 was attached. At Newcastle A1 No 2575 was put on; leaving Newcastle 51 minutes late, it arrived 57 minutes late at Edinburgh. March 1939 was a disastrous month for the 'Coronation'.

On the 13th, A3 No 2747 replaced A4 No 4902 at Doncaster on the up train and was barely 5 minutes late into King's Cross. On the following Wednesday, No 4491 was removed from the up train at Tweedmouth and replaced by C7 No 2205 which gave place to A3 No 2595 at Newcastle. The 268.3 miles to London were run in 229 minutes (225 minutes net). Two days later No 2507 worked up from

The Canadian Pacific Railway presented Dominion of Canada *with one of their locomotive bells, but after a mechanical failure which caused the bell to ring all the way to York, it was rendered inoperative.*
H. N. JAMES

A close-up of the nameplate of Dominion of Canada, *emphasising the clean lines of Eric Gill's sans serif design of lettering.*
H. N. JAMES

Newcastle in 227 minutes (222½ minutes net) at an average of 72.3 mph for the whole 268.3 miles. Driver Nash and Fireman Gilbey of King's Cross were responsible for these two fine runs.

Although few observers could see the down 'Coronation', many made it a solemn ritual to be at their local vantage points every night to see the train come up, before repairing hastily to bed. Not often were they disappointed by late running. Oakleigh Park was a good vantage point. Here the approaching train could be heard leaving Hadley south tunnel, then the two dimly lit headlamps were seen rounding the curve from New Barnet before she swept past at speed. On those nights when the driver was A. J. Taylor, OBE, there would be two long blasts on the chime whistle as he approached, giving due notice to his wife that he would be home by ten past eleven! (His home was adjacent to Oakleigh Park station.) Apart from us enthusiasts, it was common for local residents returning late from the City on the local train arriving Oakleigh Park at 10.11 pm., to wait on the platform until the 'Coronation' had gone.

The 5.12 pm Broad Street to Potters Bar, then operated by the LMSR using 0–6–0T 'Jinties', ran on the slow line from Finsbury Park to New Barnet non-stop. This was a favourite train for 'City Gentlemen' homeward bound, and it was a source of great wonder to the casual traveller to find that these otherwise staid gentlemen, lowered their evening papers after emerging from Barnet tunnel. They gazed anxiously out of the off-side windows until the man nearest the window announced 'Here she comes' and all heads turned to view the 'Silver Jubilee' sweep by in all its glory.

At Helpston, north of Peterborough, where the former Midland line to Stamford and beyond runs parallel with the GN main line, there was a station on the MR line. One summer evening the LMS station master was seen to usher out his wife and family, all of whom then stood on the up platform waiting to see the 'Silver Jubilee' pass by – a remarkable tribute from a man belonging to the rival concern!

One morning the daily papers headlined a story about a new British fighter aircraft flying from Turnhouse (Edinburgh) to Northolt in just under one hour. The same afternoon King's Cross driver Charlie Peachey and his mate signed on at Top Shed to take the 'Jubilee' to Newcastle. Nothing was said about planes or the like

as they set about preparing the engine. In due course they reached Fletton Junction where steam was shut off for the customary slow passage through Peterborough. Charlie pulled out his watch and shouted across to his mate 'That chap would have been in Edinburgh by now!'

On 4th September 1936, No 2510 failed at York on the up 'Jubilee' and was replaced by poppet valve C7 No 732. Leaving York at 11.31 am, the train reached Doncaster in 35 minutes. Driver Samwells stopped at Doncaster in the hope of obtaining a Pacific, because he said 'To have continued with No 732 would just about have killed the fireman'. The only replacement available was an Ivatt Atlantic No 4452, which was accepted. The ensuing 156.0 miles to King's Cross were covered in 139 minutes, start to stop, an average of 67.0 mph. This represented a gain of 3 minutes on the pass-to-stop schedule of 143 minutes. On another occasion, No 2510 was replaced at Peterborough by two Atlantics, but details are lacking. On 19th January 1937,

the up train was worked throughout from Newcastle by A3 No 2503. Driver Payne arrived at King's Cross one minute early on this occasion. On two successive days in April 1937 the train was in trouble. On the 13th a hot box on one of the coach bogies caused the train to stop at Corby Glen, where one unit was removed. The spare set, made up of four ordinary coaches, plus a triplet dining car set, left Wood Green about 9.30 pm behind Atlantic No 4403. This set did a double trip on the 14th, when the down train failed at Browney Colliery because No 2512 blew a gland. G5 0–4–4T No 1752 was provided by Durham to work the train on to Newcastle, reached 48 minutes late. On 22nd/23rd July, 1939 the solitary W1 4–6–4 No 10000 worked a double trip on the 'Jubilee' with driver Sheen, who arrived back at King's Cross right time on the return trip.

The 'West Riding Limited' was worked exclusively by King's Cross engines and men. A special link was created for the purpose, known as No 1A Leeds Lodge

Empire of India heading the down 'Coronation', passing Welwyn Garden City. The undeveloped state of the Garden City in prewar days is noticeable.
L & GRP

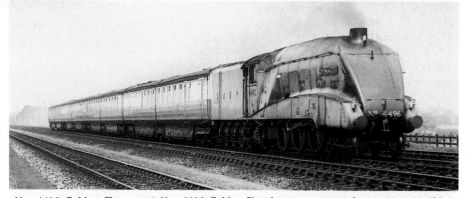

No. 4495 Golden Fleece *and No. 4496* Golden Shuttle *were reserved for working the 'West Riding Limited', and it was unusual to see any other locomotive on this duty, or one of this pair on the other streamline trains. Here* Golden Shuttle *is seen heading the up 'West Riding Limited', at Corby in 1939.*
H. C. DOYLE

Link and consisting of six sets. Two sets worked to Leeds each week. The first commenced on Sundays with the 6.0 pm express from King's Cross (6.20 pm in summer) returning on the 'West Riding' on Monday. The second set went down on the 'West Riding' on Monday, Wednesday and Friday, returning on the up train the following days, except on Saturdays when they worked the 10.0 am ex Leeds. The first set, of course, went down on Tuesdays and Thursdays, returning on Wednesdays and Fridays. The Bradford portion of this train was worked to and from Leeds by two tank engines, usually N2s, but sometimes by an N1 and N2.

It was not unusual for the 'West Riding' to be taken down by the A4 which had arrived from Newcastle with the up 'Jubilee' the same day, or for the up 'West Riding' engine to go down on the 'Jubilee'. However, commencing on 13th March 1939, revised engine diagrams resulted in the King's Cross A4s working the 7.25 am King's Cross–Doncaster (arrive 10.26 am), then 12.45 pm back to King's Cross (arrive

3.47 pm) before taking out the 'West Riding' at 7.10 pm. This gave a mileage of just under 500 in one day.

On 14th January 1938, the down train was taken by V2 No 4789 following a failure by A4 No 2512 after attachment to the train at King's Cross.

All three streamlined trains made their last journeys on Thursday, 31st August

1939. the 'Silver Jubilee' was worked by No 4489 (up) and No 4499 (down), the 'Coronation' by No 4487 (down) and No 4488 (up), the 'West Riding Limited' by Nos 4495/6 which were on the up and down trains respectively. So, as the lights went out over Europe, the brilliant concept of the Gresley streamlined trains was gone, never to return.

Headboards were not employed on the streamline trains. Here is the 'Coronation' leaving Platform 5 at King's Cross on 19th April 1938. The locomotive is Dominion of New Zealand.

L. HANSON

LOCOMOTIVE WORKING WITH THE STREAMLINERS

JOHN F. CLAY

TODAY we have some very fast trains in Britain and the members of our Society, although mainly interested in steam, will not wish to denigrate the prowess of the Deltics and the 25kV electrics. With modern motive power, train speeds have now passed beyond the point where it could be said that 'given a strong fireman' steam could have done just as well. No so many years ago, however, in the 1950s and pre-Deltic 60s, it was possible to look back with disbelief at the memory of steam trains reaching Newcastle in 4 hours, Edinburgh in 6 hours and Leeds in 2 hours 43 minutes. Yet it was true that during the years 1935–1939 such trains really did run. In relation to the science of the period the Gresley streamliners were an achievement every bit as creditable as the best that is produced today.

In the mid-1930s there was a stirring in railway offices the world over. Road competition was having its effect and the menace of internal air lines, which could seriously threaten railway receipts, lay just over the horizon. In Germany and the United States there had been the first experiments with diesel traction. At first these high speed diesel trains were little more than light rail-cars but the potentiality was showing itself. Steam engineers made their replies with the streamlined 05 class 4–6–4s in Germany and the Hiawatha Atlantics in the United States. Towards the end of 1934, Mr H. N. Gresley, as he then was, forecast a new pattern of steam-hauled trains with light high-speed expresses taking the cream of the traffic while heavy trains at medium speeds dealt with the bulk of the passengers. Such a policy had been advocated by C. Rous Marten following the fast run by the GWR 4–4–0 *City of Bath* with the Royal Special in 1903 and again by the late Cecil J. Allen in 1919 who advocated a $6\frac{1}{2}$ hour schedule to Edinburgh for a special 250 ton train worked by East Coast Atlantics and a similar service on the West Coast to Glasgow. Gresley's paper of 1934 was the first support these enthusiastic writers had ever received from a responsible railway officer.

The first high-speed diesel service to go into operation was the German 'Flying

A rudimentary form of streamlining, intended to assist smoke deflection, was applied to the first P2, No. 2001, Cock o' the North, in its original form. It was on trial from King's Cross for several months when new, and is seen here in the locomotive yard at King's Cross station.
COLLECTION A. B. COLLINS

Hamburger', a streamlined two-car set which commenced operation on a daily schedule of 77.4 mph start to stop in 1933. The Berlin-Hamburg line was admirably suited for high-speed running as it was straight and level for almost all of its length. Towards the end of 1934 the LNER management, impressed by the German train, requested an examination of possible schedules for a similar service in this country. The reply of the German engineers was disappointing as the speeds reached daily over the north German plain could not be repeated over the LNER gradients. Test runs were made using steam power, first with No 2750 *Papyrus* to Newcastle and back. The first British 100 mph maximum speed, supported by a dynamometer car record, was attained by 4472 and a sensational 108 mph by 2750. Here was clear evidence that steam power could match the times of contemporary high speed diesels with greater comfort for the passengers in a conventional train. The decision was made to build a high-speed steam train for service on a 4 hour King's Cross–Newcastle run in the autumn of 1935. It was to be called the 'Silver Jubilee' in honour of 25 years of reign by King George V and Queen Mary.

It must have needed prodigious effort to produce the drawings and build the

engines and coaches in such a short time, but thoughts of enthusiasts in the summer of 1935 dwelt on the possible form of the new engine. Would it be a Pacific version of *Cock o' the North*? We know now that at first it easily might have been. Others thought that perhaps the Atlantic would be revived following the lead of the Chicago, Milwaukee, St Paul and Pacific with their Hiawatha engines. One old timer, who worshipped the memory of Patrick Stirling, even hoped for some Gresley singles! The external form of the streamlined casing of No 2509 *Silver Link* was a bit of a shock, but a technical description revealed that the changes from the well-tried A3 design were relatively small but soundly based. It was impossible, within our restricted loading gauge, to use the large driving wheels of 7 ft diameter of the CM St P & PRR Atlantics or the 7 ft 6 in of the German 05 4–6–4s. Although this was perhaps a slight handicap for high speed pure and simple, it was an advantage when the streamlined engines were used on ordinary express services.

On Friday, 27th September, the new 'Silver Jubilee' train, consisting of engine No 2509 *Silver Link* and two articulated twins and a triplet dining car set weighing 230 tons, was given its famous dem-

A classic combination of locomotive and train, Silver Link *heading the up 'Silver Jubilee' at Potters Bar.*   RAS MARKETING (PHOTOMATIC)

onstration run when Peterborough was passed in 55 minutes 5 seconds for the 76.4 miles, 43 miles were covered at an average of 100 mph, 70 miles at an average of 91.8 mph and a maximum of $112\frac{1}{2}$ mph was reached at Arlesey and again at Sandy. Only in the previous March we had been impressed by the 108 mph maximum of *Papyrus*, now *Silver Link* had averaged $107\frac{1}{2}$ mph for 25 miles. The run had been somewhat wild for the passengers as some of the curves had not then been fully super-elevated and the new stock was rather lively on its springs but it soon settled down to a reasonably high standard of riding in everyday service.

The impact of the new train was all that the publicity people could have wished. Modern research has shown that the actual benefit of streamlining at the speeds required for normal running was less than at first claimed from experiments with models but the publicity value was immense. Many people thought that the new shape meant exotic new ideas of internal design, but coal tests against A3 class engine No 2503 showed little difference in consumption although it was announced that the A4 had proved to be 4lb/mile more economical. The A4, however, could obviously be pressed to higher horse-powers and higher speeds than the A3 if required. The new train was a great attraction even to people not normally interested in railways. The homeward bound suburban trains, overtaken by the down 'Silver Jubilee' leaving King's Cross at 5.30 pm, were travelling grand-

stands of interested spectators, while in Grantham the men in one of the clubs in the winter of 1935 stopped the billiards and tale telling and as time came round to 5 minutes to 7.00 they would listen until the chime whistle was heard, then watches would be consulted and normal activities resumed. The fox-hunting news of the local weekly paper recorded that the Belvoir Hunt emerged from a fox covert near Barkston in time to see the new 'Silver Jubilee' train also in full cry. The train was also the subject of a religious feature conducted by a local vicar.

After the exciting events of the demonstration run, normal running was well within the capacity of the engine. For the first fortnight, *Silver Link* carried the burden alone, running from Newcastle to King's Cross and back each day until the second engine *Quicksilver* was run in and ready to share the work. During the first week some heroic repair work was done to the brick arch at Gateshead Shed and Gresley was shocked that men had to work in such uncomfortable conditions when 'a green Pacific' could easily have done the job. The publicity department would not have relished the absence of the silver engine just when all eyes were on the train. When the full set of four A4s was in service, three were kept at King's Cross and the other, No 2511, was standby engine at Gateshead. The engine that took the down 'Silver Jubilee' on Friday evenings returned to King's Cross on the up 'Scotsman' the next day. Many enthusiasts who were at work during the

week sought out the 'Scotsman' in order to photograph the A4s on the Saturdays. It was soon apparent that the new engines had just as much mastery over the 'Scotsman' loaded to perhaps 16 bogies of 550 gross tons as they had with the high speed streamliner.

In August of 1936 test runs were made with the dynamometer car added to the 'Silver Jubilee' train and 113 mph was reached by No 2512 *Silver Fox* on the descent from Stoke. It was not, however, an event which reflected much credit on the responsible authorities in that the driver was not warned that a high maximum was required until the last minute. This meant that, without a preliminary build-up, the engine had to be opened out unduly hard to get the required speed and the middle big end overheated. In order to avoid disappointing the reporters awaiting the arrival at King's Cross, they kept going and the result was a big end completely disintegrated and a cylinder head pushed off. The full story of the near disaster was kept well hidden and was only revealed after the war. The return journey was much better in that a maximum speed of 90 mph was enforced, but the uphill work was of a high standard although the engine was not driven unduly hard. The test showed that an A4 had a considerable margin in hand with the normal load.

The 'Silver Jubilee' was the most successful of the LNER streamliners from the point of view of both reliable running and commercially. It was not until 4th September 1936 that a failure on the road needed a replacement engine. In this case a former GNR Atlantic made a valiant effort from Doncaster to King's Cross in 139 minutes. The first failure of the coaching stock took place in April 1937 when a stop had to be made for a hot box. 72% of the down journeys were made on time during the first two years and 68% of the up runs. The average lateness was only $2\frac{1}{2}$ minutes going down and $1\frac{3}{4}$ minutes coming up. If one or two abnormal delays were excluded, the average lateness, in all weathers, was $1\frac{1}{2}$ minutes. These figures are taken from an official press release in 1937 but unofficial platform-end observers in 1938 reported that the 'Jubilee' was only once late into King's Cross on a day of thick fog, between 27th October and 25th November. The train carried a high proportion of its seats filled and during the first year's working gross receipts were 13s 11d per mile and operating expenses 2s 6d per mile. From the supplementary fares alone, 35% of the capital cost of £34,500, a contrast to the

high cost of today's equipment, had been paid in the first year.

It was perhaps inevitable that the success of the Newcastle streamliner should direct attention towards the provision of a similar service to Edinburgh and in September 1936 the standby engine from Gateshead worked north with the 'Silver Jubilee' set and the dynamometer car to test the possibilities of the Newcastle–Edinburgh route. The engine only needed to be extended on the Cockburnspath Bank which was climbed at 64–65 mph. This involved an ihp of 2500–2600 which, to the delight of LNER enthusiasts, was slightly higher than the 2450 hp published by the LMS as the maximum hp of their Pacific No 6201 *Princess Elizabeth* on its high-speed test run to Glasgow and back in November, 1936. The LMS test runs had been made in the knowledge that they would have to match the proposed LNER high-speed train to Edinburgh. The excitement of the 1895 Races to Scotland was revived to some extent by the prospect of this competition in prestige and it

was heightened by the news that the LMS were to build an improved Pacific for their streamlined train. 1937 promised to be an exciting year.

The LNER high-speed train to Scotland went into regular service as the summer timetable started in July 1937. It was named the 'Coronation' and consisted of four articulated twins and beaver tail observation car. The whole was finished in garter blue with light blue upper panels while the engine was also in garter blue with red wheels. It was a handsome train weighing 325 tons with passengers, and full advantage had been taken of the reserve power which the A4s had shown on test with the 'Silver Jubilee'. It was timed to run to Edinburgh in 6 hours, with a stop at York going north and at Newcastle coming south. The LMS replied with the 'Coronation Scot' to Glasgow, hauled by an enlarged and improved streamlined Pacific. It had a load of nine bogies of unstreamlined stock but which were painted blue with continuous white lines from the front of the engine's streamlined

Each of the 'Commonwealth' series of A4s was the subject of an official naming ceremony. Until this took place, the nameplates were covered, as in the case of No. 4488 Union of South Africa, *seen heading the 10.50 a.m. slow train to Peterborough, near Cemetery Box, New Southgate, in June 1937.*

ERIC NEVE

Union of South Africa *again, before its name was unveiled, on an outer suburban working at Platform 15, King's Cross.*
COLLECTION A. B. COLLINS

casing to the rear of the train. On a test run on 29th June the LMS train reached a speed at least equal to *Silver Fox's* 113 mph but which was publicised as 114 mph on the slender evidence of a speedometer reading. The return journey from Crewe was made in 119 minutes for the 158 miles with a load of 270 tons as one kitchen car had been dropped from the load. The following day the LNER 'Coronation' was given a press run and there was some disappointment that No 4489 *Dominion of Canada* only reached $109\frac{1}{2}$ mph, although this was a reasonably good performance with 325 tons. The LNER was facing its most potent competitor.

In ordinary service, however, the 'Coronation Scot' offered no great challenge. Traditional LMS policy had imposed some caution and the schedule of $6\frac{1}{2}$ hours to and from Glasgow could be maintained with ease by the new Pacifics with no speeds higher than 83–85 mph. The LNER 'Coronation', on the other hand, was given a similar timing to the lighter 'Silver Jubilee' over the GNR section despite its heavier load. The booking of the down train to York was 157 minutes start to stop or an average speed of 71.9 mph start to stop, which took the British record from the GWR 'Cheltenham Flyer' over the 77 easy miles from Swindon to Paddington. This booking could be kept by an A4 but with a slender margin against permanent way delays. On some of the best runs Stoke Bank was topped at 70–75 mph with an average of 80–81 mph from Tallington to the summit. Cecil J. Allen claimed that such

uphill work was not matched anywhere in Britain at that time, a claim which no partisan challenger succeeded in disputing. In ordinary service, however, a speed of 65–66 mph was the more usual minimum as drivers found that a few seconds dropped on the climb could easily be recovered before York. The engine was working through to Edinburgh and an evenly sustained effort was wiser than high individual power outputs followed by easings. A late arrival of 5 to 10 minutes at York could usually be recovered by Edinburgh.

The difficulty of the southbound schedule lay in the fact that the maximum effort came at the tail end of the run when the fireman, working through from Newcastle, was tiring and the coal supply was declining. There was little or no margin for recovery south of Grantham. On one or two occasions the coal supply ran out completely in bad weather and an Atlantic had to be taken as pilot from Hitchin, but partisans should note that similar happenings befell the 'Coronation Scot', once as far north as Nuneaton. One of the fastest times to York by the 'Coronation' was made with maximum speeds no higher than $89\frac{1}{2}$ mph but with high speeds uphill. On other occasions speeds as high as 107 mph on the descent of Ripton Bank and of 106 mph on the descent from Stoke were recorded. The general tendency was towards higher downhill but lower uphill speeds than with the lighter 'Silver Jubilee'. The coal consumption on a normal run was said to be 43 lb/mile as against 37–39

lb/mile with the lighter train. Such figures would not have been unduly heavy for an ordinary express at 55–60 mph but on a train which covered so many of the miles in 40–45 seconds it meant brisk work with the shovel. The margins were tight for men and machines, especially as the number of electric generators for cooking, lighting and air-conditioning made coach resistance greater than that on the same tonnage of ordinary corridor stock.

In the post-war world there have been those who thought that the Gresley streamliners had 'good timings on paper'. In actual fact the standard of time-keeping was remarkably high especially when it is remembered that there were still wayside stations, stopping trains and loose-coupled freights using the main line. There were railway officers who disliked the flyers because of the difficulty of threading them through the ordinary traffic with double block sections kept clear in front as a safety measure. During the months of April and May 1939, the down 'Coronation' was only twice late at Newcastle and one of these late arrivals was only one minute behind time.

The late R. E. L. Charlewood, a former LMS officer, who was once described by Cecil J. Allen as the most careful recorder he had ever known, timed twenty runs on the 157 min booking from King's Cross to York. The latest actual arrival time was 4 minutes 41 seconds late after severe signal checks near Biggleswade; the slowest net time was two minutes over the booking owing mainly to unduly cautious observation of the service slacks. The fastest net time was 154 minutes or three minutes under the booked time. On five runs out of the twenty, speed was over 70 mph at Stoke Summit but the general average was 65–67 mph. Two of the runs had maximum speeds of 100 mph or over but time could be kept with nothing over 90 mph. Mr Charlewood also timed seventeen runs in the up direction with a booking of 237 minutes from Newcastle; with the exception of one run which involved an engine failure, the latest actual arrival was again $4\frac{1}{2}$ minutes owing to signals near Cadwell, while the fastest net time was $231\frac{1}{2}$ minutes or $5\frac{1}{2}$ minutes under schedule. One run only topped Stevenage at 70 mph and one had a 100 mph maximum. For a random sample these show a high general standard of running.

In the Autumn of 1937 the third streamliner, the 'West Riding Limited', was intro-

Dominion of Canada *starting the down 'Coronation' from Platform 8, King's Cross. The onlookers on Platform 10 were probably deafened by the blast from the outsize Canadian whistle.*
COLLECTION A. B. COLLINS

One of the two observation cars constructed for the 'Coronation'. These were not used in the winter months, when almost all of the down journey was made after dark.
LNER

duced between King's Cross and Leeds in 2 hours 43 minutes. A new link of drivers was recruited from the King's Cross fast freight services and these men soon showed themselves in no way inferior to the more senior men in the Newcastle link. In fact some of the best runs ever recorded on the streamliners took place on the 'West Riding Limited'. The up train followed the up 'Silver Jubilee' from Doncaster to King's Cross and usually had a good road, but the down train, leaving King's Cross at 7.10 pm, ran into some evening freight services and was subject to more delay. The load was eight vehicles, similar to the 'Coronation' but without the beaver tail coach. The shorter distance and the lighter load imposed no special problem to the locomotives as compared with the 'Coronation'. After March 1938 the task of the up 'Coronation' was eased by the relaxation of the speed restrictions over the automatically signalled Darlington to York section which allowed three more minutes over the tightly timed GNR section. The 'West Riding Limited' then became the hardest up booking. It was observed at King's Cross on twenty-two occasions during May 1939, five times early, thirteen times on time and 2–3 minutes late on the remaining four trips, and this was during a period when a good deal of relaying was taking place.

The full story of the LNER streamlined trains can best be shown in tabular form:

Empire of India *heading the down 'Coronation' past Potters Bar on 2nd September 1937.*
H. C. DOYLE

'West Riding Limited'
No 4498 *Sir Nigel Gresley*, 295 tons, King's Cross–Leeds, 185.7 miles, 156¾ minutes actual.
No 4493 *Woodcock*, 295 tons, Leeds–King's Cross, 185.7 miles, 155 minutes net.
No 4498 *Sir Nigel Gresley*, 295 tons, Leeds–King's Cross, 185.7 miles, 158 minutes actual.
No 2555 *Centenary* (A1 later A10), 295 tons, Leeds–King's Cross, 185.7 miles, 162½ minutes actual.
No 4789 (V2), 295 tons, King's Cross–Leeds, 185.7 miles, 167 minutes net.

There were admittedly a number of failures which allowed green Pacifics to show their capacity for high-speed running. The two fastest runs of the up 'Coronation' were indeed to the credit of A3 class

Name	Distance miles	Av. speed mph	Load (Tons) Vehs/Tare/Loaded
'Silver Jubilee' (up and down)	232.25	70.4	7/220/230 until 3/38
'Silver Jubilee' (up and down)	232.25	70.4	8/248/265 after 3/38
'Coronation' (down)	188.15	71.9	9/312/325 summer load
'Coronation' (down)	188.15	71.9	8/278/295 winter load
'Coronation' (up)	268.25	68.0	9/312/325 summer load
'Coronation' (up)	268.25	68.0	8/278/295 winter load
'West Riding Limited' (down)	185.70	68.4	8/278/295
'West Riding Limited' (up)	185.70	67.9	8/278/295

There were, of course, a number of individual runs which involved a measurable gain on scheduled times. Among the most notable net times are the following:

'Silver Jubilee' (down)
No 2509 *Silver Link*, 230 tons, King's Cross–Darlington, 232.25 miles, 194 minutes 40 seconds, 187¼ net.

'Coronation' (down)
No 4496 *Golden Shuttle*, 325 tons, King's Cross–York, 188.15 miles, 154 minutes 35 seconds actual.
No 4488 *Union of South Africa*, 325 tons, King's Cross–York, 188.15 miles, 154 minutes net.

'Coronation' (up)
No 2595 *Trigo* (A3), 295 tons, Newcastle–King's Cross, 268.25 miles, 230 minutes, 225 minutes net.
No 2507 *Singapore* (A3), 295 tons, Newcastle–King's Cross, 268.25 miles, 228½ minutes, 222½ minutes net.

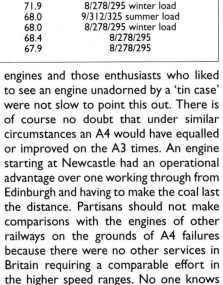

engines and those enthusiasts who liked to see an engine unadorned by a 'tin case' were not slow to point this out. There is of course no doubt that under similar circumstances an A4 would have equalled or improved on the A3 times. An engine starting at Newcastle had an operational advantage over one working through from Edinburgh and having to make the coal last the distance. Partisans should not make comparisons with the engines of other railways on the grounds of A4 failures because there were no other services in Britain requiring a comparable effort in the higher speed ranges. No one knows how others would have fared under the same conditions.

There were many occasions when exceptional efforts were recorded over portions of the journey, notably on the climb to Stoke Box. The fastest climb of all would appear to be an average of 84.7 mph from Tallington to the summit by *Silver Link* with the 230 ton 'Silver Jubilee', while a climb by *Empire of India* with the full 325 ton 'Coronation' averaged 81.1 mph from Tallington with a minimum of 74 mph which would have required an ihp of about 2300 sustained for 12 minutes. *Dominion of New Zealand*, with the up 'West Riding Limited', made the fastest climb to Stevenage on record with an average of 86.6 mph from Arlesey to Stevenage and a minimum of 81½ mph at the summit. This formed part of a run from passing Doncaster to King's Cross in 122 minutes 29 seconds with two 100 mph maxima, at Crow Park and (101) at Essendine. The double-chimneyed engine No 4901 *Capercaillie* made a sedate run apart from a burst from Huntington to Hitchin in 17 minutes 55 seconds pass-to-pass, an average of 90.3 mph against the rising tendency of the road. No 4491 *Commonwealth of Australia* on the down 'Coronation' averaged 79.8 mph for the 156.7 miles from Hatfield to Selby pass-to-pass with three separate 100 mph maxima. The highest speed, apart from the officially sanctioned 113 mph test performance of *Silver Fox* on the up 'Silver Jubilee' was 107 mph by *Golden Plover* down Ripton Bank on the down 'Coronation'. There were a number of speeds in the 100–106 mph range and 90 mph speeds were easily maintained on level or slightly rising grades.

With hindsight we can make a number of criticisms of the operating. It would perhaps have been wiser to have changed engines at Newcastle on the 'Coronation'. Greater reliability might have been gained at some cost in mileage. It would seem that insufficient use was made of the very efficient engines fitted with Kylchap exhaust. Only one of the four, No 4902 *Seagull*, was at King's Cross and able to take a share in the streamlined workings, although No 4901 was borrowed from Gateshead for a few trips. Two were at Doncaster taking turns on duties well within the capacity of a green Pacific or a V2, and No 4903 *Peregrine*, an excellent engine, never had a trip on a streamliner. If the 'Coronation' had been largely handled by these four, then things might have been better. A very high standard of reliability had been obtained on 'Silver Jubilee' with the original selected engines, but as economy was sought with higher mileage and cyclic workings, the failures mounted, as could be seen by the number of times when emergency substitutions had to be made in 1938/9. The stream-liners had such an effect on the LNER image that the craving for mileage seems false economy. In any case, although impressive figures for individual engines were published, the mileage record of the A4 class as a whole did not show any very exceptional merit. It might well have been possible to have given special treatment to the engines of the high speed trains with little adverse effect on the overall figures. The exceptional performance of the contemporary Chapelon Pacifics and 4–8–0s in France was not accompanied by high mileage figures.

Nevertheless, the LNER pre-war streamliners represent such a praise-worthy phase in British railway history that it seems churlish to criticise. Even the single-chimneyed A4s could hardly be described as sluggish. Writers are largely agreed that the performance of the A4s during the years 1935–39 showed the British steam locomotive at its most superlative level. The combination of high speed, load and distance demanded higher standards than were ever required of steam in this country. The effect of the high-speed trains was an upsurge in internal morale and external prestige just at the time when the railways needed a better image. The Gresley streamliners set standards for the East Coast route, and at a time when some other regions seemed content with Type 4 diesels, the Eastern Region realised that only Deltics were adequate for the demands of the 1960s.

No. 4468 Mallard *approaching Grantham with the 1.30 p.m. from King's Cross to Hull on 30th July 1938. Driver Duddington, who was at the regulator when this engine achieved 125 mph, can be seen at the cab window. The locos rostered for the streamlined trains came from King's Cross and Haymarket sheds, and as Mallard was shedded at Doncaster, it missed out on the regular streamline running.*   JOHN F. CLAY

The streamline Pacifics were once unkindly compared to a stranded whale. Perhaps this head-on view of double-chimney No. 4902 Seagull *provides an excuse for such irreverence. The location is Tempsford on 17th July 1938 in the course of brake trials.*   H. M. HOATHER

Silver Link in its early days skirting Durham City, with the imposing bulk of the cathedral as a backdrop. The LNER were ambivalent in their use of the definite article in association with their named trains, but this is clearly 'The Silver Jubilee'.
DURHAM COUNTY ADVERTISER

THE 'SILVER JUBILEE' – A DAY TO REMEMBER

MICHAEL JOYCE

THE year 1935 saw many important events. Baldwin succeeded Mac-Donald as our Prime Minister; Italy went to war with Abyssinia and there was a plebiscite for the return of the Tsar to Germany. It also brought more pleasant events, and one of these was the Silver Jubilee of King George V and Queen Mary. This was celebrated in many ways throughout the country, but it also heralded the beginning of a five-year period in our railway history the like of which has not been seen since.

Rivalry between the East and West Coast Routes for supremacy in the Anglo-Scottish service had been steadily growing, and in November 1934 the LNER, under H. N. Gresley, had shown its intentions in no uncertain manner by making high speed runs between King's Cross and Leeds, and back, followed early in 1935 by two further runs to Newcastle, and back, to prove that a four-hour service to that important North-East city by a steam hauled train was not only possible, but could be a reality. And so, in early September 1935, the LNER introduced to the public a fully streamlined train, painted silver, and a locomotive of startling appearance. It, too, was fully streamlined and painted silver, and carried the name *Silver Link*. The train was to provide a regular four-hour service between King's Cross and Newcastle and, appropriately, was named 'Silver Jubilee'. The effect on the public was dramatic, and on none more than myself in common with all railway enthusiasts.

I was only 15 at the time, living in Leeds, and 1935 had already become a landmark in my life for I had started work in March. Although Doncaster was less than 30 miles south of Leeds, and York under 25 miles to the east, the opportunities for seeing this new engine and train were slender. It cost money to travel, and with a wage of five shillings a week and pocket money of only a shilling, it was out of the question. However, my dreams were to be realised in a most unexpected manner in January 1936.

Working as an office-boy for a privately-owned oil company, I had access to a typewriter, copy paper and carbons, and during my lunch hour I produced a modest news

Dominion of Canada *was occasionally used on the 'Jubilee', and is seen here passing Werrington troughs with the down train on 25th July 1939.*
H. C. DOYLE

sheet on railway matters which circulated through the office and works – selling for one old penny a time! Imagine my shock and fear when I was sent for by the owner of the company and asked to explain the private venture!

Surprisingly, my boss was not angry (I had feared the sack), and seemed genuinely interested to learn of my hobby. Before I left his office he had announced that I was to be given a day off work and provided with tickets to travel from Leeds to Darlington and then on to King's Cross and back. This was not, however, to be an ordinary journey, for seats had been reserved on the 'Silver Jubilee' express to London, and similar reservations on the 'West Riding Pullman' back to Leeds! Enough money to cover meals on both trains went with the tickets.

So it was, on a cold January morning in 1936 I stood on the windy platform at Darlington waiting for the arrival of the up 'Silver Jubilee'. I had never been so far from home, and I felt somewhat intimidated by the other waiting passengers who, being much older, appeared to exude a confidence that I could not muster. The anticipation was agonising and the excitement hard to conceal!

Shortly before the 'Jubilee' was due, another southbound express came into

the station and I could not believe my eyes – a streamlined Pacific was at its head, my very first sight of one of the finest engines ever to be built in Britain. It was the Gateshead-based *Silver King*, normally used as the 'stand-by' for the King's Cross engine that would work the streamlined train. This sight, alone, would have been enough to make my day, but shortly afterwards the 'Silver Jubilee' steamed majestically into the dreary, draughty station and my mind was fully occupied with finding my coach and seat amidst the scurry and bustle of passengers and station staff anxious to get on board and the train away on time.

Memories of that journey to King's Cross are somewhat vague, and were at the time. Everything was full of exciting new sights and sounds. I had managed to note that the engine at the head of the train was 2510 *Quicksilver* but, after I had found my seat at the corridor side of a 3rd Class compartment, time flashed past as quickly as the train passed through stations. I remember the passage through York which seemed to be only a few short minutes after I had joined the train at Darlington, and before long a call for lunch saw me wending my way to the dining car. I had a chance to wonder at the luxury of the first class coaches, and to sit in the

Silver King *passing Peterborough North with the up 'Silver Jubilee', probably in 1936.*   T. G. HEPBURN, RAIL ARCHIVE STEPHENSON

magnificently appointed dining car. I could not say what I had for lunch, nor what its cost was, but I would imagine that I would have parted with something in the region of 5/- for a three-course meal!

On my journey back to my seat I recall seeing a speedometer fixed to a panel in one of the first class coaches and that the train was travelling at 85 mph. Where this was I cannot say; perhaps running down Stoke bank. It was all a fantastic kaleidoscope of sights and sounds that made clear thinking an impossibility.

Far too quickly, or so it seemed, we were pulling into King's Cross, my very first visit to this Mecca of LNER enthusiasts and I was soon carried along the platform surrounded by other passengers. I had little chance to get close to *Quicksilver* for there was a crowd of press photographers intent on getting their indi-

vidual shots of a young man who, I learned later, was Crown Prince Olav of Norway who had been travelling in the 'Jubilee'. He had come over to represent his country at the funeral of King George V who had died a few days before. Not only had I travelled on the 'Silver Jubilee', but a 'Royal Train' to boot!

My day was far from being over. I carried a letter from my boss for the King's Cross station master, and I made my way to his office. The letter contained a request that I might be shown some of the workings of that terminus before I returned to Leeds on the Pullman. I was placed in the hands of an Inspector who took me to the end of No 10 Platform and then across the tracks to the station locomotive depot. There in all its glory stood *Quicksilver* under the coaling chutes. From the ground the Pacific seemed massive, and I was

invited to climb up into the cab. To me, a boy of 15, it was unbelievable. It was hard to take it all in, and when coaling had been completed we slowly moved backwards on to the turntable and, as I sat in the fireman's seat, the engine was turned. It moved off into a reception road and, before I left the footplate, I was able to stand inside the corridor tender and was given a description of the various engine controls. My stay with *Quicksilver* came to an end too soon, and I left it to be prepared for its return run to Newcastle before I was shown round the all-electric signal box and my own return home.

In a lifetime of railway experiences and memories, that day is one that stands out more sharply than any other. I saw the 'Jubilee' on many other occasions but never made another journey on that wonderful train.

THE ANONYMOUS YEARS

DAVID LOWTHER

DURING the war years, the 'Silver Jubilee' set was stored and exercised at intervals to maintain its serviceability but the end of hostilities did not see its return to high speed service for neither the tracks nor the locomotives were in any condition to resume fast running.

Early in 1948 strong rumours began to circulate that the 'Silver Jubilee' was to return to service, but they were sad days for Britain's railways and when the new train materialized on 27th September 1948, it turned out to be another addition to the Pullman fleet with the title of 'Tees–Tyne Pullman'. In view of the rolling-stock shortage, the streamline trains were split up and the 'Silver Jubilee' twin-first (Sc1581/2E) and triplet-third (Sc1586–8E) were despatched to the Scottish Region early in 1948. The restaurant-triplet (E1583–5E) fared better and, based in the North Eastern Region, ran in the principal Newcastle to King's Cross services, starting with the 8.15 am service in mid-1948. The set received no special treatment but merely shared the duties with the other Gresley triplet-restaurant sets. Like them, its fate was decided by its kitchen equipment, for from 1959, new BR restaurant car deliveries with propane gas cooking facilities, resulted in the wholesale withdrawal during 1962/3 of the LNER all-electric kitchen stock favoured by Gresley. It operated in the 9.53 am Newcastle–King's Cross and 5.35 pm return during 1960, but further new deliveries made it redundant at Heaton, and on 18th August 1961, it was stored in the west bay at Manors station with one of the 1938 'Flying Scotsman' triplet-restaurant sets (E1428–30E). These sets were to remain together, being towed to Tyne Dock in 1963 for final destruction with other LNER restaurant vehicles. By May of that year, with interiors wrecked and prepared for 'firing', the end was near. I was able to pay my last respects, but too late to salvage any fittings. It was, however, evident that others had appreciated the comfort of the first class restaurant armchairs for the gateman's hut was splendidly adorned with one!

No. 60047 Donovan heading the 5.35 p.m. down Newcastle, near Hawkshead bridge on 5th September 1953. The one-time 'Silver Jubilee' triplet restaurant car set can just be discerned in the centre of the train, by this time repainted in BR 'blood and custard' livery. G. W. GOSLIN

In Scotland in 1948, the five passenger vehicles (Sc1581/2E, 1586–8E) were maintained as a set for the summer only 'Fife Coast Express' and the winter un-named Glasgow to Leven working. The former departed from Glasgow Queen Street at 4.7 pm and, with stops at Burntisland Kirkcaldy, Leven, Elie and Anstruther, St Andrews was not reached before 6.53 pm. In the city-bound direction, the 'Fife Coast Express' was away from St Andrews at 7.15 am and, without the Burntisland stop, reached Glasgow by 9.50 am. The nameless winter working was even more humble for it ran as the down express to Leven only and there was no corresponding return service.

However, these five coaches were still given special treatment during their visits to Cowlairs Works. In BR livery, no lining was applied to the body sides for the raised polished metal strips were retained, and the train always kept its distinctive appearance. After the introduction of diesel multiple units in the mid-1950s, the coaches were relegated to stopping and

relief services from the Glasgow area but they rarely ventured south.

Shortly before withdrawal, twin-BFK, Sc1581–2E, appeared in the 5.37 pm (Fridays Only) Manchester Exchange–Newcastle on 17th August 1962. This brief reunion with the East Coast main line terminated on 20th August 1962, when Sc 581–2E worked back to Glasgow in the 9.30 am (Mondays Only) from York. This was to be the final chapter for in 1963 the coaches were broken up, having rested for some months in a tremendous dump of coaches in Ardmore sidings, east of Craigendoran station. Some rapid correspondence saved two of the armchairs, delivered to York, carriage free, for £1!

Had the coaches survived a further three years, no doubt more would have been preserved from the fine train but their non-standard equipment and seating layout caused their demise, leaving little but photographs, logs and other splendid memories to serve as a record of a remarkable service.

H. N. Gresley's second Pacific, in original condition. It was to be named Sir Frederick Banbury, after the chairman of the Great Northern Railway, who was a vociferous opponent of the grouping, and refused to accept a position on the LNER Board.

REAL PHOTOGRAPHS

PACIFIC LOCOMOTIVE DEVELOPMENT

HOW GOOD WERE THE ORIGINAL GRESLEY PACIFICS?

JOHN F. CLAY

IN the early 1950s, in a magazine mainly concerned with railways other than the LNER, a writer made the seemingly heretical claim that the older engines with short lap, short travel valve gear were just as good as those built later and incorporating the ideas adopted by Churchward. He based his argument on examples of the older types running successfully on short cut-offs and cited the Adams and Pettigrew trials on the LSWR in 1891 when an Adams 4–4–0 reached 80 mph downhill with 636 ihp on 17–18%, and the trials on the Caledonian in 1889 when the Drummond 4–4–0 No 79 developed 552 ihp at $65\frac{1}{2}$ mph on 19% cut-off.

He had faithfully reported the published results but his argument was from the particular to the general, although nevertheless it could have been reinforced by unscrupulously selective quotation. For example the figures of 3.63 lb/dbhp/hr for an NER Class Z Atlantic, 3.64 for a Midland Compound and 3.64 for a Claughton, could have been compared with 3.79 lb/dbhp/hr by No 5000 *Launceston Castle* on the LMS in 1926 and 3.74 by No 6018 *King Henry VI* on its own line in 1948. No untrue figure has been quoted but they are misleading by being incomplete. It has been conveniently forgotten that, on other occasions, a 'Castle' recorded 2.83 lb/dbhp/hr and a 'King' 2.81, while the three earlier classes, on other occasions, had given results of 4.5–5.

While the argument has been overstated, the point has been established that, when the engine was in good condition and everything was steamtight, some of the older engines could, on individual occasions, do surprisingly well. There is a case for closer examination to find if there are any elements of truth in the short lap case with special reference to the viewpoints expressed by LNER apologists for the disappointing early performances of the Gresley Pacifics, especially after the events of 1925.

It was argued, in quite high LNER circles, that as No 4474 on the GWR had decreased its coal consumption in lbs/mile, especially in the up direction, as the trials progressed, a longer period of testing might have brought its consumption down to the GWR figure. This is an argument with some elements of validity, but it has obvious absurdities if taken too far. It might be asked, for example, by GWR partisans, how long it would have taken to reduce coal consumption to nothing. It was, however, a valid argument that, in view of the comparatively good performance of 4474 on the GWR in 1925 and the test results of Nos 1472/3 on the Doncaster–King's Cross road in 1923, better performance might have been expected from No 2545 on its own road in 1925.

It has been suggested that the original Gresley Pacifics were inhibited by the men persisting with their traditional methods of driving the GNR Atlantics with long cut-offs and partially opened regulators. It has been asked if the Pacifics might have performed better with wider regulator openings and shorter cut-offs, which would have been possible even with their original valve gear. It has further been suggested that, in the late 1920s and early 1930s, Pacifics which retained short lap valves took turns with the modified engines and made good runs for which they got no credit.

Today there is no need to have any doubts about published runs because the RCTS Part 2A book gives the dates on which valve gears were modified, and runs made in the 1928–30 period may be properly assessed. The following table of best runs by unmodified engines is not claimed to be exhaustive but it is hoped that it is reasonably representative.

that they were in the later 1930s. All the runs were later excelled, often by a wide margin, by 180 lb Pacifics with long lap gear, but these modified engines had not shown their full power or speed capacity by 1931 when the last Pacific was modified. Even so, it is hard to imagine the accelerated bookings from 1932 onwards being worked with success by unmodified engines.

It is unfortunate that there were fewer runs recorded from the footplate in the 1920s than was the case in the 1930s. The earliest evidence we have of the way Pacifics were worked comes from the late Cecil J. Allen's footplate run on No 1473 in 1923 and the published results of the tests of 1472/3 against the NER No 2400 in the same year. In all cases cut-offs of 40–45% were used uphill and downhill. Downhill speeds and dbhp's were low, and low steam chest pressures were used with long cut-offs. On one run, described in *Gresley Observer* No 46, the average dbhp from King's Cross to Knebworth was 819, but it was only 337, a figure well within the capacity of a Stirling 8-footer, from Knebworth to Peterborough. Obviously, however, no 8-footer could have recovered from 40 mph near Ouse Box, Huntingdon, up 1 in 200, to 45 mph near MP62 as did the Pacific with its 560 ton train.

The first indication that some drivers were adopting different methods of handling Pacifics was published by Cecil J. Allen, in the September 1925 *Railway Magazine*, when he described a run by No 2582, with 455 tons, on an easily timed Edinburgh to

Engine	Load, tons	From	To	Miles	Min Sec	Date of publication
4471	536/580	King's Cross	Peterborough	76.4	81.24	Aug. 1925
4471	536/580	Peterborough	Grantham	29.1	36.00	Aug. 1925
4472	494/525	King's Cross	Peterborough	76.4	78.27	3rd June, 1927[1]
2543	565/600	Peterborough	King's Cross	76.4	84[2]	Dec. 1926
4470	318/340	Grantham	King's Cross	105.5	$103\frac{3}{4}$[3]	June 1929
2561	390/415	Grantham	King's Cross	105.5	$105\frac{3}{4}$[3]	Nov. 1928

[1] Date of run. [2] Guard's journal timing. [3] Net time.

The first conclusion is that heavy load runs are more impressive than those at higher speeds with more moderate tonnage, but they all took place at a time when high speeds were not needed to keep the GNR line schedules to the extent

Newcastle run. No 2582 climbed Cockburnspath on the usual 45% but on the easier sections it was run on 30% uphill and 20–25% downhill. In the December 1928 issue, Mr Allen described a run, timed from the footplate by the late

No. 2547 Doncaster, a right-hand drive A3.

R. A. H. Weight, on the 10.15 am down. No 2562, with its Type E superheater but still retaining its short lap valves, ran a 485 ton train to Peterborough in 81¼ min. Cut-offs were 40–45% up to Potters Bar, but 25–28% sufficed for the rest of the run. The continuation to Grantham took 36 min 30 sec with cut-off increased from 30% at Werrington to 40% at Stoke summit. Grantham to Doncaster took 51¾ min. net with cut-offs of 25% increased to 30% up to Markham summit.

While these runs represented some advance on the traditional methods, it emerges that, when hard uphill work was required, the same 40–45% cut-offs were needed. When shorter cut-offs were used, speeds and dbhp's were relatively low. It did not represent true expansive working as practised in 1925 on the GWR or as was to become LNER practice in the 1930s. In 1935 O. S. Nock rode on No 4476, with long lap valves, hauling 515 tons against 485 tons with No 2562, and a faster climb was made to Stoke on 25–28% cut-off than the short lap engine made on 30–40%. It is obvious that all disappointments with the earlier engines cannot realistically be ascribed to heavy-handed driving. A certain amount of coal may have been saved by linking up downhill but it is unlikely to have been more than marginal. The progressively reduced consumption of No 4474 on the GWR could have been due to a greater familiarity with the difficult twists and turns of the road.

The point of cut-offs is only one factor in overall locomotive efficiency and there is evidence that an engine with the more modern gear could produce a high efficiency on comparatively long cut-offs. The problems of wire drawing and excessive back pressure affected efficiency more on earlier designs. The New York Central J3 Hudsons, with an enormous boiler in relation to their cylinder capacity, were estimated to give a drawbar thermal efficiency of 6.1% compared with a corresponding 6.25% for a Gresley A3 Class Pacific (*Loco. Profile* No 2, page 38). The J3s worked loads of up to 1,550 tons on 59 mph schedules over a mainly level route with cut-offs as long as 40% at 80 mph and 60% at 65 mph. They were, however, designed with such hard work in mind, with the freest possible flow of steam when worked with such vigour for hours on end. It is not intended to imply that the hand-fired Gresley Pacifics should have emulated these giant mechanically-fired

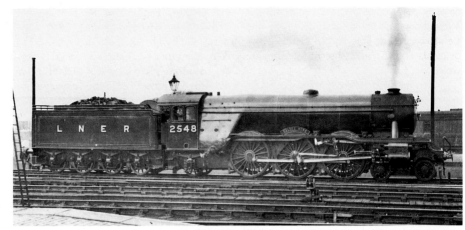

No. 2548 Galtee More, *rebuilt with long-travel valves but retaining its original 180lb boiler pressure, was one of the Great Northern section stalwarts in the 1930s, and is seen here at its home base of Grantham.*
JOHN F. CLAY

locomotives, but merely to reinforce the idea that the ability to pass large volumes of steam through valves, pipes and ports was vital to the success of any locomotive.

It would appear that the original Gresley Pacifics passed only a limited volume of steam through their valves even when worked hard on 40–45% cut-offs. The highest calculated ihp which can be credited to one, for a distance long enough to be significant, was just over 1600 for 17 min between Newbury and Savernake during the 1925 exchange. It gains some confirmation from the best edbhp of 1365 by No 1473 on test detailed on page 44 of *Gresley Observer* No 46. The maximum claimed for 'Castle' No 4074 in the 1924 trials was also 1600. The highest calculated figure which can be ascribed to 'Castle' No 4079 on the LNER was 1400 with a possible 1450 with a bit of special pleading. No 4079 was, throughout the tests, well on top of its LNER schedules, so the unfortunate No 2545, losing time on the same schedules, was hardly producing more than 1100–1200 ihp. Such a figure was often required in 1925 from the various Atlantics, by D10 and D11 4–4–0s and by B12 4–6–0s. Clearly there were more things wrong with 2545, possible valve leakage among them, than have been identified. The indifferent performance should not, without more evidence, be blamed entirely on poor handling.

The best Pacific runs on the LNER would in 1925 have needed hp's much closer to those of 4474 on the GWR; in fact No 4471, taking its 580 ton load up Stoke, would require an ihp so close as to lie within the margin of error which must be given to all calculated hp's. Both engines almost certainly must have needed 40–

45% cut-offs with fairly wide regulator openings. The boiler, stimulated by the fierce blast, must have supplied the necessary steam for 15–20 min but the figure of 17 ihp/ton of engine weight is unremarkable – such a figure was possible many years earlier from a Stirling 8-footer or 2–2–2. Seventeen ihp per ton was, however, close to the national average. It is doubtful if a Stanier Pacific, in its original form with low superheat, ever did any better, yet the Kylchap A4 and the Duchess Class Pacifics, developed from the original LNER and LMS Pacifics, were demonstrably capable of 25–27 ihp/ton for comparable distances.

One of the most valuable qualities of the original Gresley Pacific was that it was capable of future development. The transformation from short lap to long lap valves cost only £150–£190 per locomotive, for which modest sum a more free-running machine emerged, which produced similar work on about 40 lb of coal per mile against 50 lb. To have improved the Raven Pacifics in the same way would have involved a complete rebuilding in which little of the original engine would have survived in a hardly recognisable successor (page 25, *East Coast Pacifics at Work*, P. N. Townend, Ian Allan, 1982).

The improved performance which came with the various stages of development of the Gresley Pacific design can be shown numerically over the same stretch of rising gradient. No 4902's run in the following table was made after two years of war. Higher ihp's were recorded by Kylchap A4s at higher speeds with lighter loads such as the occasion when *Mallard* topped the bank at 78 mph with 415 tons. The runs in the table are, however, more directly comparable. The 78 mph run by *Mallard* involved an ihp of 2785 which was a considerable advance on 1600 ihp for the originals for a modest increase in engine weight.

Tallington – Stoke Box 15.3 miles

4471	A1 original valve gear	536/580 tons	17 min 50 sec
4477	A1 modified valve gear	520/560 „	16 „ 20 „
2501	A3	533/570 „	15 „ 32 „
4490	A4 single chimney	593/635 „	15 „ 49 „
4902	A4 double chimney	608/660 „	15 „ 38 „

Despite their shortcomings, the Gresley Pacifics, as built, were useful assets to their owners but their merit came from their size rather than their quality. They were able to work very heavy loads on the schedules which were acceptable in the early 1920s, and during the 1926 coal strike the LNER was in the best position of any British railway to run exceptional loads on imported coal. The refined GWR 'Castles' lost much of their sparkle during the same emergency, and the inadequacy of the Midland 'small engine policy' for the West Coast main line was further emphasised, and impetus was given to the chain of events leading inexorably towards the introduction of the 'Royal Scots' in 1927.

The superior speed capacity of the long-lapped 180 lb Pacifics was demonstrated quite early. The highest maximum speed which can, reliably, be credited to an orig-inal Gresley Pacific was 88 mph by No 2557 near Bytham with 280 tons, described by Mr Allen in December 1928. A maximum of 90 mph with 310 tons at the same spot by a C1 Atlantic was published in June 1929. Speeds attained on the level are of more significance than those reached downhill and records of over 70 mph were recorded by both Gresley and Raven Pacifics on the Darlington to York section, but rarely, if ever, were their best efforts beyond the best achievements of the C7 Atlantics. In October 1930 Mr Allen described a run by No 2569, with modified valve gear, hauling 290 tons; a maximum of $88\frac{1}{2}$ mph was reached on level track near Tollerton. This was far beyond any NER engine and was quite as good as anything recorded up till then on the GWR. It was an indication of what might be expected from the modified Pacifics.

There is no doubt at all about the benefits to the Gresley Pacifics following the adoption of long lap valves. This was of the order of a reduction in coal/dbhp/hr of 25–30% while the engines were stronger and faster. The only valid conclusion emerging from a defence of the short lap case is that the importance of steam-tight valves was established. It may be that some percentage of the demonstrable improvement in Pacific performance was due to the contemporary reduction in valve leakage. This is supported by LMS experience, slightly later, with the 'Royal Scots.' There is insufficient evidence to attempt a numerical assessment of the extent to which reduced steam leakage affected the final overall result. Such indications as there are suggest that it was in no way sensational. The most valuable effect of improved steam tightness was greater consistency of performance. The old style broad ring valves gave good performance when first fitted but leakage increased as the time for shopping drew near. This again is supported by LMS experience. The original Gresley Pacifics may have been deficient in some points of detailed design but they were admirable in their general conception and they proved to be capable of successful development.

Bibliography:

British Locomotives at Work, O.S. Nock, Greenlake Publications, 1947.
Locomotives of the LNER, Part 2A, RCTS, 1973.
East Coast Pacifics at Work, P.N. Townend, Ian Allan, 1982.
Various issues – *The Railway Magazine, The Gresley Observer, Locomotive Profiles, S.L.S. Journals*

Sir Hugo, the last of the batch of twenty Pacifics built by the North British Loco Co. in 1924, spent most of its life allocated to Heaton shed. Here it is seen at Darlington in 1947, evidently not long after repainting in LNER livery, bearing its new number in traditional block characters.

RAS MARKETING (PHOTOMATIC)

EARLY RUNS WITH THE ORIGINAL PACIFICS

ERIC NEVE

WRITING in the journal of another society some years ago, a well-known commentator, referring to the variable standard of driving and firing encountered in the early years of the LNER Pacifics, stated that 'Gresley must bear most of the blame'. This completely ignores the fact that from the date of his appointment as Chief Mechanical Engineer of the LNER, Gresley ceased to have responsibility for locomotive running. This devolved on the locomotive superintendent of each area, the position in the Southern Area being held by W. G. P. Maclure, formerly of the Great Central Railway. Consequently, it may be felt that he, and his district inspectors, ought to accept much of the blame. Likewise, it is still unexplained how the two King's Cross drivers, Glasgow and Pibworth, came to be selected for the 1925 exchanges. Going by the seniority list, neither was senior at the time, but it is noticeable that Glasgow was given the first Pacific to operate from King's Cross shed in 1922. From Monday, 24th July onwards, the engine and driver worked mainly on the 10 am and 10.10 am expresses from London, until 1471 returned to Doncaster shed on 23rd October. Then, in 1923 when 4474 and 4475 were allocated to King's Cross, they were booked to Glasgow and Pibworth respectively. We may infer from that that these two drivers must have been highly regarded by somebody. It has been said recently by one of the few surviving members of Gresley's staff that these same two were selected for the 1925 trials by the Assistant Running Superintendent, King's Cross. Furthermore, it has also been stated by a man who fired to Driver Glasgow that Gresley once rode with them down to Grantham and remarked that the engine had not been worked in the manner it should have been, but performance and coal consumption had been good!

Incidentally, in regard to the brief visit of *Pendennis Castle* to Doncaster shed before the trials commenced, this occurred on Thursday, 23rd April 1925 when the engine and GWR crew took the 10.10 am

Leeds express down from King's Cross to Doncaster (arrival 1.08 pm). It then spent about 13 hours on the Carr loco shed before being prepared for the return journey to London, starting at 4.24 am on the Friday. As the booked working of these trains normally was for a Doncaster engine and crew to work the 4.24 am Aberdeen sleeping car train up to London and return with the 10.10 am, we may conclude that on 23rd April the Doncaster Pacific remained at King's Cross while the crew conducted GWR Driver Young on the 10.10 am so that he could have a sight of the road before the trials commenced.

It might be said that this sojourn on Doncaster shed by 4079 was arranged on purpose to provide the 'unexpected opportunity' for examination of its valve gear. We shall never know I fear, but I do think that if Gresley instructed Doncaster to proceed with the proposal to fit a Pacific with long travel valves, under the date 23rd April 1925, he must have decided *before* the clandestine examination took place. Otherwise the date quoted in RCTS Part 2A has been misread.

We now know that Bert Spencer, one of Gresley's assistants at the time, rode on the engine to London during the tests but with Driver Tomblin. As drivers did not usually make London trips on successive days, we can assume that two drivers were involved and what Gresley said to Spencer would have been for coal consumption by the other driver in the *tests*, i.e. Tomblin, (The link would have contained at least ten drivers at that time, possibly twelve.) Incidentally, Tomblin took 4480 regularly following its rebuilding to A3 in July 1927.

One of the late R. A. H. Weight's notebooks, which I was able to acquire shortly after his death, quotes several instances of performances by short-lap A1s in their early days. The first run, not tabled here, was on 25th July 1922 behind 1470, then about three months out of shops, on the 12.02 pm ex-Doncaster, due King's Cross at 4 pm. With 390 tons, Driver Buxton of Doncaster was seen off by Mr Gresley amidst considerable interest shown by railwaymen and other spectators. The

50.5 miles to Grantham were run in 58 minutes (schedule 60) without much exceeding 60 mph. The next stage on to Peterborough, 29.1 miles, started with a 'full cry' climb up to Stoke, passed at 44 mph in 10 minutes for the 5.5 miles. Down the bank a maximum of 74 mph was reached and Peterborough reached in $32\frac{1}{2}$ minutes (34 allowed). Through coaches from Grimsby were attached there, bringing the load up to 450 tons to be hauled up to London in 86 minutes. A fine start was made, passing Huntington in less than 21 minutes (22 schedule) after which things were taken easily. Stevenage summit was breasted at a minimum of 41 mph. After a maximum of 60 mph Hatfield was passed a minute early and then a severe slowing for signal repairs at Marshmoor kept speed down to 47 mph at Potters Bar. Touching 72 mph before New Southgate, King's Cross was reached only a few seconds behind time in $83\frac{1}{4}$ minutes net. About five minutes had been gained by the engine on the through run, easily. Long cut-offs were used and there is no doubt that in these early days steam pressure was often lower, and coal consumption higher, than they should have been.

Run A in the tables took place in October 1923 with the same driver working 1479N, then only three months old, on the accelerated Leeds–London 'Breakfast Train'. This run demonstrated to Mr Weight the practicability of 60 mph bookings with moderate loads over the GN main line. As will be noted, several delays were encountered. The train started from Doncaster $5\frac{1}{2}$ minutes late, reduced to $4\frac{1}{2}$ at Retford, afterwards achieving even time by reaching Grantham (33.1 miles from Retford) in 33 min 10 sec. The climb up to Stoke was less impressive than that up the 1 in 178 to Markham and soon after a severe p.w.s. at Essendine spoiled the descent following a maximum of $80\frac{1}{2}$ mph. On the level through Connington, 74 mph was attained and $61\frac{1}{2}$ mph minimum up Ripton bank brought them through Huntingdon a few seconds early. Then over the 34 miles up to Knebworth an average of $65\frac{1}{2}$ mph was maintained. More delays were then encountered and

Another regular GN section performer, No. 2559 The Tetrarch, passing Potters Bar with an important down express in the 1930s. GRESLEY SOCIETY COLLECTION

King's Cross reached 2½ minutes late, but 13½ minutes had been lost through delays and the net time from Grantham was only 104 minutes.

Run B describes Mr Weight's first trip down from London behind a Pacific loaded to over 500 tons on the 5.40 pm West Riding express. There was some slipping through the tunnels up to Holloway; a slack through Barnet tunnel and a p.w.s., together causing Hatfield to be passed two minutes over schedule but the ensuing 34 miles on to St Neots occupied only 32 minutes. Another slack over the Ouse bridge outside Huntingdon and an easy finish to Peterborough put them 1½ minutes down arriving. Net time was estimated as 83½ minutes against a schedule of 87.

The last run, C, took place five years later and was Mr Weight's last long-distance footplate trip, on the 10.10 am ex-King's Cross. The 490 ton gross load included the unique quintuple restaurant car set that operated on this train for many years. Coal was described as poor and very dusty. The engine was sluggish out to Potters Bar and in getting away from Peterborough. The regulator was half closed following the ascent to Leys summit beyond Huntingdon, otherwise it was full or 7/8ths open.

In studying these logs I wonder whether Mr Weight thought the Doncaster drivers made a better job of handling the Pacifics than the London men. I would like to have seen at least one run with Driver Glasgow for comparison. The log book also contains two very fine runs behind Doncaster Driver Charlie Molson and his famous 'Super' Pacific No 2544 *Lemberg*, one on the 'Breakfast Train' in very adverse weather and with a load 100 tons above normal. The other was with no less than 565 tons on the down 'Scarborough Flier' when some very trying delays were had.

Date: October 1923 RUN A
Driver: Buxton
Engine: 1479N Load: 280/295T

Miles			Schedule	Actual	Speed
0.0			0	—	
17.4	Retford	arr.	20	18.56	
	,,	dep.	0	0.00	
4.6	MP134			7.15	54
18.4	Newark		20	18.30	72½
33.1	Grantham	arr.	37	33.10	
	,,	dep.	0	0.00	
5.5	Stoke			8.37	48½
16.9	Essendine			18.41	p.w.s.
29.1	Peterborough		31	31.22	20
46.6	Huntingdon		50	49.44	
61.4	Sandy			62.57	65/70½
73.6	Hitchin		77	74.00	59½
80.5	Knebworth			80.50	65½/73
					p.w.s. 20½
87.8	Hatfield		92	89.55	
92.8	Potters Bar			95.05	57
					p.w.s sigs
101.4	Hornsey		105	103.00	
105.5	King's Cross	arr.	111	112.00	

Date: June 1923 RUN B
Driver: Horton
Engine: 1470N Load: 481/510T

Miles			Schedule	Actual	Speed
0.0	King's Cross	dep.	0	—	
2.6	Finsbury Park			7.30	35
12.7	Potters Bar			21.16	42
				p.w.s.	25
17.7	Hatfield		25	27.00	—
23.5	Woolmer Green			33.55	47 min.
31.9	Hitchin		40	42.10	
				p.w.s.	
58.9	Huntingdon		67	67.45	
62.0	Stukeley Box			72.20	51
76.4	Peterborough	arr.	87	88.15	(rain)
	,,	dep.	0	0.00	
8.5	Tallington			11.58	60
12.2	Essendine			15.40	57
23.6	Stoke			29.37	41
29.1	Grantham	arr.	37	36.05	

Date: 1928 RUN C
Driver: Kershaw
Engine: 2562 Load: 459/490T

Miles			Schedule	Actual	Speed	Cut-off %	Pressure
0.0	King's Cross	dep.	0	—			
2.6	Finsbury Park			6.45	32	35	165
12.7	Potters Bar			21.05	40	28	165
17.7	Hatfield		25	26.20	66	25	
31.9	Hitchin		39	39.55	75	25	
58.9	Huntingdon		64	62.10	69/66	25	
62.0	Stukeley Box			65.25	51 min.	25 eased	
76.4	Peterborough	arr.	83	81.00			
		dep.	0	0.00		65	
12.2	Essendine			16.00	54	30	165
23.6	Stoke			30.40	41 min.	35	
29.1	Grantham	arr.	36	36.50			
		dep.	0	0.00		50	
9.9	Claypole			11.35	72½/69	25	175
14.6	Newark		16	15.45	68/70	25	
26.4	Tuxford			27.40	47	30	170
33.1	Retford		35	34.55	68	25	
45.8	Rossington			46.30	66	25	170
50.2	Bridge Jc.			50.55	sig. stop		
50.5	Doncaster		54	54.55			

No. 4479 Robert the Devil heading a down Leeds express through Sandy with the LNWR lines and signal box to the left.

G. H. SOOLE

GRESLEY PACIFICS AND SUPER-PACIFICS

NORMAN NEWSOME

IT must be remembered that the breaking of speed records was not the only ambition of the Board of the LNER and its chief officers, as they were intent on producing a better railway with higher average speeds for the more important services, and Gresley was anxious in his capacity of Chief Mechanical Engineer to improve the efficiency of the locomotives and rolling stock for which he was responsible. It was therefore not surprising that following the lack of success of the LNER in the locomotive exchanges with the GWR in 1925, Gresley wanted to improve the efficiency of his locomotives to give lower coal consumption. He therefore consulted his chief technical assistant, Bert Spencer, who at that time was at King's Cross with Gresley, and the result was that Spencer produced a design for modification to the locomotive valve gear. A new design was also prepared by Doncaster Drawing Office. The design was also prepared by Doncaster Drawing Office. The design prepared by Spencer was fitted to No 2555 *Centenary* and the Doncaster design was fitted to another locomotive (No 4477 *Gay Crusader*). Extensive tests were carried out between Doncaster and King's Cross on the 8.40 am from Doncaster and the 1.30 pm from King's Cross, with the result that coal consumption of 2,555 came down to about 35lb per mile, which was much better than anything which had been achieved previously including the trials with the GWR. The tests with 2555 were carried out with the engine under the jurisdiction of Driver W. Tomblin and Fireman Richmond of Doncaster depot and also with another set of Doncaster men. I travelled many times on this locomotive between Doncaster and London and it was surprising to see how little coal was consumed on that round trip of more than 300 miles. It was also interesting to note that when the Doncaster men were in control, the regulator was opened fully after starting and it was not touched again until the train had to stop. Any variations in the power required from the engine was dealt with by alteration in the cut-off which, for much of

the journey, remained at 15% and on one occasion I saw it down to 12%.

As a result of the success of these tests, all the LNER Pacific locomotives had their valve gear altered in accordance with Spencer's design and this became the standard for all new engines including of course all the streamlined ones which worked the 'Silver Jubilee'. Reference to this alteration in the valve gear was made by O. S. Nock in his book entitled *Locomotives of Sir Nigel Gresley* on page 44, and on page 132 he tabulates the steam chest pressures and cut-offs which illustrate how efficiently the engine was being operated. All the locomotives which took part in the experimental runs were fitted with

modified valve gear as he used on No 2555.

It must be borne in mind that before and after the advent of the 'Silver Jubilee' the maximum speed normally permitted on the LNER was 90 mph and special permission had to be given before this was exceeded. It was not intended that this maximum speed was to be exceeded when the 'Silver Jubilee' went into regular service, and Gresley never failed to emphasise that the reduction in journey time was brought about by rapid acceleration and by running fast uphill. In his presidential address to the Institution of Mechanical Engineers, he made reference to this and drew attention to the fact that

One of the first batch of Pacifics built as A3 class, with 220lb per sq inch boiler pressure, No. 2747 Coronach approaching Sandy with an up Leeds express. A Doncaster-based engine for most of the 1930s, it was later to be a regular performer on the Waverley route in Scotland.
G. H. SOOLE

An evocative view of No. 2582 Sir Hugo leaving York for the south on 22nd August 1937. The North Eastern Railway was noted for the complexity of its signalling arrangements, which were progressively simplified in LNER days.   H. C. DOYLE

No. 4480 Enterprise *was the first Gresley Pacific to be fitted with the 220lb/sq inch boiler and classified A3 as a result. Here it is seen entering King's Cross, during the period in the 1930s when it was regularly seen on trains between Doncaster and the capital.*   S. FREESE

A1 class No. 4475 Flying Fox *and the later A3 No. 2743* Felstead *awaiting departure from King's Cross in 1938. The smokebox blister covering the superheater header on* Felstead *indicated the 220lb/sq inch boiler of the A3 class, and the pipe to the smokebox blower shows that the engine was driven from the left-hand side.*   S. FREESE

increasing the average speed from 60 to 90 mph saves five minutes over 15 miles, whilst to increase the speed from 30 to 60 mph saves 15 minutes over the same distance. In this address he also paid tribute to his staff at Doncaster who designed and built the 'Silver Jubilee' locomotive and train in the short period of five months.

The maximum speed of the 'Silver Jubilee' in normal service applied also to the high speed trains built later for the services to Leeds and to Edinburgh, and all the streamlined engines which worked these trains were equipped with the French 'Flaman' speed recorders fitted under the fireman's seat. The records taken from these instruments were regularly examined and if any driver exceeded 90 mph without special authority he was required to give an explanation. In fact the speed limits for various parts of the line were not exceeded in normal service.

In thinking of the events which took place more than 50 years ago I have often wondered whether they would have been so successful if the tests with the GWR had not taken place and if Gresley had not altered the valve gear on all his Pacific locomotives. It is interesting to note that in tests carried out by BR in 1948 with various types of locomotives, the LNER

Pacific locomotives on the Leeds–King's Cross service were more economical in coal consumption than the GWR 'King' type engines on the same route.

I would especially commend to all readers the descriptions given by George Dow in his book *British Steam Horses*, as the pages from 110 onwards have special significance and great interest to all in his description of the run with the 'Silver Jubilee' train before it went into regular service.

Mallard on what is believed to be the 4.00 p.m. to Leeds, climbing Holloway bank, meanwhile being diverted to the slow line.   COLLECTION A. B. COLLINS

EXAMINING THE PISTON VALVES OF A 'CASTLE'

TERRY MILLER (Introduction by the Editor)

IT has been reported on more than one occasion that the opportunity was taken by LNER staff to measure the valves of a GWR 'Castle' when one of the class was unattended by its own crew, and in the custody of the LNER. This occurred twice, in May 1925 when *Pendennis Castle* featured in the locomotive exchanges, and again when *Windsor Castle* was at Darlington for the centenary celebrations. I asked our Vice-President, Mr Terry Miller about the feasibility of the task, and he has written as follows:

'I have never heard at first hand from anyone who was engaged in this operation, but I believe it to have been perfectly feasible. It would have been necessary only to remove one piston valve from its steamchest to measure the effective width of the heads (i.e. between steam and exhaust

edges) and also the distance between the two heads (steam edge to steam edge) and then to measure the width of the ports in the steamchest and the distance between them (steam edge to steam edge) and, of course, to record all these measurements.

'The valve travel in full forward gear could easily be measured with a footrule 'on the job' while the engine was moved forward a full half turn of the coupled wheels – for safety's sake moved by being pinched along, not pushed or moved by its own steam!

'When I was in Doncaster Carr Sheds in 1932 there was an allocation of 15 Pacifics; each of them was brought into the repair road once a month without fail to have its three pistons and three valves taken out, cleaned and inspected, new rings fitted as necessary and all reassembled on the locomotive. This was done between 8 am and 5 pm in one day by two fitters, two mates and one apprentice; if all went well we were finished by 4 pm, with an hour left to clean up tools and hands! With monthly attention of this kind, all the nuts came off easily, the crosshead cotters came out

fairly easily as a rule, the piston-rods were parted from the crossheads with the aid of a special hydraulic device and a loud bang, and the removal of the valves presented no difficulty because their monthly attention ensured that there was no excessive accumulation of carbon which, in less favourable circumstances, could make removal very difficult.

'It is reasonable to assume that *Pendennis Castle* had had a fairly recent overhaul before it appeared on the LNER so that the men to whom the task was given of removing a valve whilst the engine was at the mercy of the inquisitive people in King's Cross or Doncaster, were not likely to have encountered any problem except perhaps their own lack of familiarity with GWR design and practice.

'So I would guess that two fitters would get a valve out in a couple of hours, do the measuring up that I have described and have everything restored to normal within another hour, leaving no trace of their insatiable curiosity, as Rudyard Kipling might have described it.'

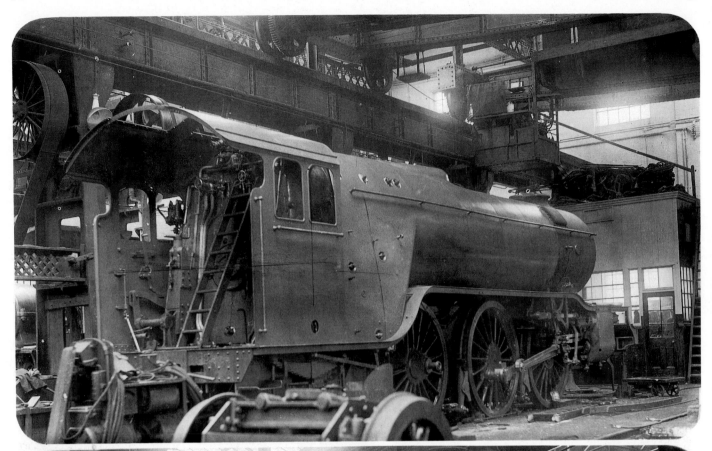

The first V2, No. 4771 Green Arrow *under construction at Doncaster Plant in June 1936. The loco first appeared as No. 637, with the nameplate attached to a dummy 'splasher', which, due to the presence of a mechanical lubricator, could not be positioned centrally.*

EDITOR'S COLLECTION

THE 'GREEN ARROWS'
THE EARLY YEARS OF THE 'GREEN ARROWS'

ERIC NEVE

V2 class No. 4780 The Snapper, *shortly after being named by the Colonel of the East Yorkshire Regiment at Hull Paragon station, on 11th September 1937. The green cylinder covers were characteristic of locos painted at Darlington.*

LNER

PRODUCTION of Gresley's new mixed traffic engine, primarily intended to replace the K3 2–6–0 design that had originated in 1920, was keenly awaited by the faithful observers in the Northern Heights. In mid-1936 they were basking in the proven success of the streamlined Pacifics but retained their interest in the more mundane matters like express goods trains! It had been expected that the new design would have 2–6–2 wheel arrangement to give improved riding at speed compared with the K3 2–6–0 'Jazzers'.

Although allocated new to King's Cross on 22nd June 1936, No 4771 *Green Arrow*, as it had so aptly been named, spent some time being thoroughly run in from Doncaster shed. At first it was on the 6.16 am stopping train to Cleethorpes, returning with the 10.50 am to Barnetby and thence 11.44 am to Doncaster. Next came a few trips up the main line leaving Doncaster at 9.00 am all stations to Grantham (7.08 am Leeds–King's Cross 'Parly'), then 11.44 am Grantham–Peterborough to return on the 3.07 pm Harrogate express (1.40 pm ex King's Cross) to Doncaster.

Green Arrow first worked up to London on Friday, 3rd July, through from Doncaster

with the 2.35 pm semi-fast due King's Cross at 6.37 pm. No time was lost by King's Cross shed in trying out their new engine as next morning it went down to Grantham with the 11.30 am York semi-fast, and returned with the first part of the 'Junior Scotsman', in the charge of a No 3 Express Goods Link crew. This provided the regular observers with their first chance to see No 4771 in action. They were not disappointed. Here was a fine looking engine, fully in keeping with the Gresley tradition, which was received with unreserved approval.

In the following week the new V2 started to work the 'Three Forty Scotsman' No 1 Express Goods (562 down) but on Saturday, 11th July, came the first double-tripped passenger duties to Peterborough and back, both Top Links turns at 7.45 am and 4.15 pm. These returned from Peterborough at 11.38 am (9.00 am ex Leeds) and 8.00 pm (5.30 pm ex Leeds) – always a heavy train. This was repeated the next Saturday, but on 25th July No 4771 went to Grantham on the 12.05 pm SO Leeds express, to return with the 3.55 pm Scottish relief, both journeys non-stop over the 105.5 miles. Later that night No 4771 went out to Peter-

borough at 10.53 pm with the Leeds part of the 10.45 express. This kind of pattern, with 562 down goods in mid-week, became established for the rest of the summer timetable.

The next four V2s were distributed over the LNER system, Nos 4772/3 to York, 4774 to Peterborough (New England) and 4775 to Dundee. No 4774 at New England at first took over the 562 Down goods from No 4771 at Westwood, working to York and returning thence at 10.20 pm with the 8.00 pm mail ex Newcastle. Often on Saturdays No 4774 came up to London with an excursion train and took back the 4.05 pm Cleethorpes express. On Sundays it came up on a braked goods, due London around 8.30 am, and went back with the 12 noon West Riding express, through to Doncaster from where the return was on a braked goods to New England. Hitherto a Grantham Pacific had been borrowed for this duty.

When the next production batch of V2s began to emerge from Darlington works in 1937, some came to Top Shed, enabling a start to be made on allocating particular engines to regular crews in No 3 Link. In this way No 4771 went to J. Burgess, No

Most of the V2s were built at Darlington, including No. 4788, here seen waiting departure from the up platform at Grantham in August 1938.
                                                                                    JOHN F. CLAY

4785 to S. Lynch and No 4789 to E. Moore, but it was not until April 1939 that all nine drivers in the link were booked to regular V2s. The additional ones were: Nos 4794 (F. King), 4797 (H. Blunt), 4816 (H. Smith), 4821 (F. Griffiths) and 4826 (H. Jarrett). Between 8.45 and 10.00 pm weeknights, four of these could be seen and heard lifting heavy loads up the long grade to Potters Bar or bringing the Hull fish down to London. Thus for a brief four-month period No 3 was the only Top Shed link to have regular engines, because the advent of streamlined trains had caused the practice to be abandoned in the higher links.

To set the scene on early performance it is useful to describe a run on Christmas Eve 1936 logged by Ray Stephenson behind 4771 on the 1.05 pm relief to the 1.20 pm 'Mid-day Scotsman' from King's Cross to Grantham. In the April issue of the 1937 *Railway Magazine* C. J. Allen remarks on this run in detail. The load was 427/455 tons and the driver W. Long, then in King's Cross No 2 Link. The start up to Finsbury Park was unusually slow (7 min 59 sec) and signals beyond New Barnet caused further delay. It was suggested the engine was sluggish, but more likely it was being held back on account of the preceding 12.54 King's Cross–Baldock slow only just ahead. This train was probably turned slow line at Potters Bar because from then on *Green Arrow* began to show its paces. After passing Hatfield $4\frac{1}{4}$ min late, Woolmer Green was topped at 60 mph and Hitchin passed at 78 mph (about 3 min late).

Speeds were 86 at Arsley, 80 at Biggleswade and 75 at Huntingdon (only 56 sec late). Peterborough was passed one minute early. After that it would seem they were running on the tail of the 2.01 pm slow Peterborough–Grantham so Driver Long did not press matters and reached Grantham in 118 min 40 sec for the 105.5 miles. Sixty miles had been run at an average of 70.9 mph, the 27.0 miles Hitchin–Huntingdon at 77.3 mph. A good enough effort indeed!

Over the difficult Harrogate–Leeds route, 4779 of Heaton, on the 10.00 am Newcastle–Liverpool, was loaded to 280 tons tare, J. W. Hague logged the best times recorded over the section up to then, 2 minutes better than the best Pacific run and a gain of $3\frac{1}{2}$ minutes on the fastest schedule. The average of about 51 mph over the $4\frac{1}{2}$ miles from Arthington, including 3 miles of 1 in 97 up, with a minimum of 30 mph at the top, was a splendid effort. The logs of both runs follow.

Distance Miles	Engine: 4771 *Green Arrow*. Load: 427 tons tare, 455 gross	Schedule Min.	Actual M. S.	Speeds mph
0.00	KING'S CROSS	0	0 00	
2.5	Finsbury Park		7 59	
5.0	Wood Green		11 44	50
9.2	New Barnet		17 47	38
12.7	Potters Bar		25 10	
17.7	HATFIELD	27	31 20	70
23.5	Woolmer Green		36 18	60
28.6	Stevenage		41 10	64
31.9	HITCHIN	41	43 57	78
37.0	Arlesey		47 35	86
41.1	Biggleswade		50 36	80
44.1	Sandy		52 56	74
51.7	St Neots		59 09	68
58.9	HUNTINGDON	64	64 56	75
62.0	MP62		67 45	60
69.9	Holme		74 02	74
75.0	Fletton Jc.		79 12	60
76.4	PETERBOROUGH	82	81 00	
79.5	Werrington Jc.		86 10	49
84.8	Tallington		92 37	49
88.6	Essendine		97 08	51
92.2	Little Bytham		101 22	47
97.1	Corby		107 53	48
100.1	Stoke		111 43	46
105.5	GRANTHAM	118	118 40	

(Courtesy R. G. C. Stephenson and *The Railway Magazine*)

Distance	Engine: 4779 Load: 280 tons tare	Schedule	Actual	Speeds
0.0	HARROGATE	0	0 00	
1.9	Crimple Jc.	4	3 03	25
3.3	Pannal		5 10	52
5.8	Weeton		8 25	66 max.
9.0	Arthington	13	10 45	54
	Bramhope Tunnel (exit)		14 15	30 min.
12.5	Horsforth	19	15 50	52
15.2	Headingley		18 30	68 max.
17.5	Holbeck	28 arr.	22 30	
		30 dep.	23 45 sigs.	
18.3	LEEDS CITY	33	30 15	

In January 1938 King's Cross driver Auger reported sick and was unable to work the 7.30 pm 'Aberdonian' sleeping car express to Grantham. No 3 Link driver E. Moore, rostered for the 9.30 pm No 1 express goods, replaced him and, probably at Moore's request, was allowed to take his regular V2 (No 4789) in lieu of a Pacific. With 530 tons, six minutes delays were recovered. A few days later No 4789 was hastily requisitioned to replace a last minute A4 failure on the 7.10 pm down 'West Riding Limited'. After a late start of 19 minutes, 13½ minutes, delays were caused by signals and 8 minutes more by three p.w. slacks – total 40½ minutes over schedule. Despite these disheartening delays No 4789 was only 38½ minutes late into Leeds, having gained 2 minutes on the exacting streamline schedule of 163 minutes for 185.7 miles (68.7 mph average), a superb effort by Driver Beach and Fireman Kirton.

Normally Doncaster V2s were not diagrammed to work south of Peterborough, but in the summer of 1939 a severe shortage of Pacifics caused them to use some of their V2s on the crack 'Yorkshire Pullman' duty to London and return on at least five occasions. Nos 4792, 4802/17/20/43 were all recorded and fortunately some runs were logged, in particular one with No 4817 driven by Jack Sherriff, reputedly the only erstwhile Mexborough GC man to attain Doncaster No 1 Link status. The load was nine Pullmans, 362/380 tons, and the schedule for the 156 miles was 155 minutes. A troublesome injector made them 1½ min late through Retford but helped by 83½ mph at Carlton, Newark was passed on time. Signals before Grantham kept speed down to 53 mph there but a steady climb up to Stoke summit was followed by remarkable speeds down the famous bank. The 3.6 miles Little Bytham–Essendine were covered at an average of 91.9 mph, 7.4 miles Bytham–Tallington at 90.2, and 17.6 miles Corby–Werrington at 86.2 mph. The maximum was estimated at 93 mph. All this was a 6 ft 2 in driving wheel mixed traffic engine! Peterborough (79.6 miles) was passed in 74 min 34 sec and, after delays at Holme, Hitchin (124.1 miles) in 119 min 41 sec. A final check at Finsbury Park meant that they reached King's Cross in 151 min 44 sec – 3¼ min inside schedule and estimated at 147½ min net. On another day No 4792, driver unknown, had an extra bogie brake added to the Pullman load, making 395/415 tons. With a strong side wind and only one signal check, at Hougham, 81 mph was attained down Stoke Bank, and King's Cross reached in 153 min 20 sec (151 minutes net). In each case these engines returned home with the 4.45 pm down Pullman, but no logs have been seen. With such performances, faith in the 'Green Arrows' was unbounded!

York, too, seemed to have a strong liking for their V2s, sending them up to London in the summers of 1938 and 1939 on Saturday reliefs to the 'Scarborough Flyer', non-stop over the 188.2 miles. On 27th August 1938, 4780 reached King's Cross at 2.25 pm from Scarborough and 4772 ten minutes later from Whitby. Both took expresses back to York next day. About this time the writer was enjoying a private visit to several running sheds in the northeast. At York the Running Foreman,

No. 4843 was one of a batch of V2s turned out from Doncaster in 1939. It had been named King's Own Yorkshire Light Infantry *in May of that year, when it was a good deal cleaner than it appears here, at Doncaster shed on 12th August 1939.*

H. C. DOYLE

Probably after an emergency, V2 class No. 60821 in charge of 'The Flying Scotsman' accelerating down Stoke bank on 19th September 1955. After nearly eight years of nationalisation, Thompson stock was still in use on this important train.

P. H. GROOM

bidding me farewell, said 'We've lost one of our V2s, if you see it anywhere tell them to send it home immediately!' But I did not see it.

With the threat of war looming large, the Saturday before August Bank Holiday 1939 was about the last occasion when lineside recorders were in their accustomed positions before the blow fell. Between 1 pm and 8 pm ten V2s worked passenger trains over the main line, four of them both up and down, such as No 4843 on the 'Yorkshire Pullman'. Later great reductions in passenger trains and elimination of fast braked goods meant V2s worked every conceivable kind of train. Many became very run down but those from Doncaster and York managed to maintain very presentable standards, and those from Tyneside too. Once I was shown how York placed a sponge cloth over the centre pin of the two to one lever to prevent ashes clogging it up. Many times a Tyneside V2 was hastily coaled and watered at Grantham and sent out to London in lieu of a Pacific. The firebox would be full of clinker and steaming poor. The Grantham crew would take it into the station loco yard at King's Cross, clean out the firebox and go home feeling very happy! One wartime exploit stands out above all others. On Sunday, 31st March 1940, the famous Gateshead Pacific *Gladiateur* arrived at Peterborough 83 minutes late with the 10.45 am ex Newcastle, loaded to 21 vehicles (603 tons tare). Five more coaches were added, bringing the load up to an incredible 764 tons tare, 850 tons full. No 2569 was replaced by V2 No 4800 with which, quite unaided, New England Driver Hensy and his mate set

V2 No. 60876 fresh from the Doncaster paint shop, on 13th May 1956.   L. HANSON

out for London, reached in 102 minutes for the 76.4 miles. The guard booked nine minutes against them but this surely must have been a feat unequalled anywhere in the country and one which never would have been contemplated by other railways. Thus was Gresley's big engine policy fully justified.

Far too much happened in subsequent years to be related here. None of us would have dreamed that in 1953 six Gresley 'Green Arrows' would be seen on the Southern Region, including 'The Bournemouth Belle' Pullman, following the temporary withdrawal of Bulleid Pacifics, or between York and Birmingham and Burton-on-Trent. As dieselisation gained momentum they made forays over many unusual routes, even to Bristol, Penrith, and on express passenger trains between Derby and St Pancras as well as to Euston

and return on local trains. Up in Scotland, too, many V2s worked over the Caledonian lines from Aberdeen to Perth, Glasgow and even the time honoured 'West Coast Postal' between Aberdeen and Carlisle.

In the south the last recorded V2 working came on 1st and 2nd November 1963 when No 60887 brought an up braked goods from Tyneside and returned with empty coaches to York. York held on to No 60831 until December 1966 and the Scottish Region actually ran a last V2 railtour from Edinburgh to Aberdeen and back on 5th November 1966 before withdrawing No 60836 in December. Those of us who remember the first workings of 4771 *Green Arrow* are happy to know that the engine has been preserved, even more so that it continues to work special trains in such a splendid manner.

MAINTENANCE OF THE 'GREEN ARROWS' IN SERVICE

TERRY MILLER

BY the time the first of the V2 Class locomotives was turned out of Doncaster Plant Works in June 1936, the first of the Gresley Pacifics, No 4470, had already been in service for 14 years and, indeed, all 79 engines of the A1 and A3 Classes had been completed and were hard at work.

The V2 engines were obviously very much of the same family as their somewhat older forebears and consequently maintenance of them was familiar to the staff in the running sheds who knew where to look for any weak spots and what was required in the way of routine exam-

inations. Furthermore, and because of the close similarity in design between the two types, modifications which had been made to the Pacifics had been embodied in the V2s and were also familiar to the maintenance staff at all the main line depots at which the new engines were likely to be allocated.

But nobody would claim that the Pacifics were without their shortcomings. Those with the greatest effect on the burden of maintenance work at the depots were the excessive wear that developed in the working parts of the conjugated valve gear, the all-too-frequent overheat-

ing of the axlebox bearings, and the overheating and not infrequent collapse of the middle connecting rod big end bearings. As far as the V2s were concerned, the heating of the axleboxes and of middle big ends though serious enough was not quite the constant headache that it was on the Pacifics. Although the repair work that they entailed was not inconsiderable, it was well within the competence of the depots so long as the resulting damage did not necessitate sending the wheels and axles to one of the main works for repair.

It was the conjugated valve gear, known as the two to one gear, that was a real

The outside valve gear and link motion of the second V2, No. 4772, in clear detail. Built at Doncaster in 1936, this loco spent all its life in the North East. LNER

worry. Unlike the B17 and D49 Class engines, in which the two to one gear was located behind the cylinders, in a nice oily, steamy and relatively clean atmosphere, in the V2s and other classes it was in front of the cylinders, just below the front of the smokebox and, worst of all, just below the smokebox door. The gear was grease lubricated and the smokebox ash which inevitably fell on to it made an effective grinding paste. The gear which actuated the piston valves of the inside cylinder had eight pin-joints in it and these, together with the bushes in which they worked, were subject to continuous wear. This in turn gave rise to the uneven beat of the exhaust which was characteristic of these engines and, at the same time, was responsible for the fact that the centre cylinder produced far more than its fair share of the power of the engine. There is little doubt that this was a contributory case of the occasional trouble experienced in the middle big ends.

In his biography entitled *Nigel Gresley; Locomotive Engineer*, the author, F. A. S. Brown, applauds the tremendous work done by the V2s and quotes many examples of their splendid performances, but he laments the abnormal wear of the pin joints of the conjugated gear, especially during the Second World War when maintenance was neglected due to shortage of qualified staff. He records that Gresley gave consideration, towards the end of 1940, to the possibility of making a major alteration to the 114 Pacifics and to the V2 Class 2–6–2s by applying conjugated gear of similar form to that used on his first three-cylinder engine No 3461, built in 1918. That engine had a two to one gear in front of the smokebox but it consisted of two shafts carrying arms of different lengths producing the required ratio of two to one. The arrangement gave excellent service although it was said that the exhaust beats were even more irregular than those produced by the simpler gear that became standard. Had the original gear been adopted, it could have been housed in an oil-tight casing at the rear of the cylinders. It was realised, however, that additional linkage would have been needed and that the O2 Class No 3461 was a slow-moving engine, very different from the high speed locomotives that followed it, and so the scheme was not developed.

Following Nationalisation in 1948, a system of preventive maintenance was adopted. Under this system all moving parts were scheduled for examination and any necessary attention after a locomotive had run a specified mileage, and this provided that at 36,000 miles the valves and pistons of a three-cylinder engine should be removed, as also should the two to one gear. So far as the V2s were concerned, the gear could sometimes be repaired at the depot, but more often it was loaded into a wagon and sent off to the main works for overhaul.

It is generally acknowledged that Sir Nigel Gresley did not take kindly to suggestions that the design of his engines should be altered. In the case of the V2 design, the boilers were so good and the steaming so satisfactory that nobody would have been wise to suggest trying to make any improvements. So it was not surprising that it was not until 1943, two years after his death, that experiments with self-cleaning smokeboxes were conducted on various classes of engines. The V2 Class in particular was tackled with fervour. The contrivance consisted of steel plates and wire mesh grids arranged in such a way as to cause smoke and unburned coal along with hot gases to be deflected to the bottom of the smokebox, round the sides of the blastpipe and finally through the wire grids before being ejected through the chimney. Theoretically this action broke up any glowing coals so that only fine dust came out of the chimney, but in fact the apparatus was not self-cleaning but only spark arresting. Six years later it was decided to fit the entire class of V2 engines, but by 1951 it was realised that the engines were not steaming freely and the fitting was stopped. There followed a whole series of further experiments until, at last, the whole thing got lost in the much more promising exercise of fitting double blastpipes. Apart from spoiling the steaming of the engines, the so-called self-cleaning smokeboxes caused a lot of unnecessary trouble in the depots. The plates and grids were supposed to be removed (temporarily) when the boilers were being washed out so that access could be gained to the wash-out plug in the front tube plates, but this was a difficult job and the boiler-washers had to try to squeeze in between the blast-pipe and the sides of the smokebox; anyone who has worked in a hot smokebox, probably half full of fine ash, will know how pleasant that was. On the other hand, there was nothing less popular with drivers and firemen than anything that interfered with the free steaming of their engines, so it is not surprising that if you knew where to look you were likely to come upon a stack of steel plates and wire mesh grids!

Splendid engines though the 'Green Arrows' were and *Green Arrow* itself still is, the engine that can never fail has not yet been built. Thus it is that an incident that had to be seen to be believed once occurred on the Up Main line a few miles north of Dundee and the author of these notes saw it for himself.

A message was received at Dundee Tay Bridge Shed to the effect that the engine working an up express fish train had failed and could not be moved. Having arrived at the scene, all the small gang sent to the rescue saw was a smart-looking V2 standing at the head of its train, simmering away quietly in the sunshine of a summer afternoon. First glance revealed nothing wrong, but a more searching look around revealed that the right-hand connecting rod was not in the attitude it should have been. Its big end was safely on the crank pin of the right driving wheel but its small end was not connected to the right crosshead. Instead it was lying on the ballast below the right front corner of the firebox. Between the big end and the small end stretched the connecting rod, completely undamaged and intact. It was, of course, upside-down! How did it get into that attitude? Yes, the gudgeon pin that should have been in the right crosshead was missing. The loss of a gudgeon pin was not unheard of, but this one had gone without trace, not even a scratch on the paint of the right leading coupled wheel through whose spokes it must have escaped. But more remarkable than this was the fact that the connecting rod had managed to get itself pointing towards the back of the engine instead of forwards and to have got there without being damaged — not so much as a scratch on it.

The only possible explanation was that when the gudgeon pin came out, the small end dropped to the ground, it and the connecting rod dug down vertically into the ballast and was pulled out again as the engine continued to move forwards. Would that all mishaps ended as happily as that — just think what *might* have happened.

MEMORIES OF No. 866

BERT COLLINS

MY short footplate career began at Top Shed in August 1947. After a spell as a cleaner I reached the age of 16, when as a novice fireman I was rostered in the 'Odd Met' link. The seniority situation at this period was such that youngsters such as myself, together with droves of ex-servicemen, were joining the railway at the same time and because of this I was able to leapfrog the lower links into the 'Odd Met' where I joined Driver Joe Holland. Joe was a member of a family of railwaymen who all worked in the King's Cross area. His bearing and aptitude for the job that he obviously loved were to be an inspiration to me.

Our partnership began one night on a turn to Feltham with one of Ivatt's N1 0–6–2Ts. Joe's opening words to me were that he did not like working on any engine unless it was spotlessly clean! Joe stood six feet tall, barrel-chested, with a gruff but kindly voice. His boots and overalls were always immaculate – an obvious legacy from his service as a guardsman in the Great War. As a result of this wartime service he lost his seniority on the Great Northern, which was why he was saddled with me in a lower link rather than in the Top Link where he rightfully belonged. I had been a 'front' wiper as a cleaner, which meant that I had some idea of how to clean the footplate controls which helped my cause as far as getting into Joe's good books was concerned. I had also gleaned a little experience with the shovel when, as the aforementioned 'front' wiper, the rostered firemen preferred me to make their fire up, rather than clean their engine! It therefore behoved Joe to try and knock me into shape as a fireman. This, I think, he eventually achieved, although only after we experienced many interesting adventures together, with me trying to keep steam in the boiler and Joe keeping his eyes on both me and the road!

As I gained more experience, Joe and I became good friends and he would relate his experiences on the 'Silver Jubilee'. I listened in awe as he told me how he would leave King's Cross on *Silver Link* with about 170 psi of steam and water just visible in the bottom nut of the gauge glasses, and by Finsbury Park the engine

would be showing three-quarters of a glass of water, with the needle on the red mark, a position that would remain throughout the rest of the trip!

After a few months in the 'Odd Met' at Top Shed, I took the decision to transfer to Hornsey as I found it difficult to get to work at King's Cross when rostered on awkward turns. I could get to Hornsey on foot in 15 minutes.

At Hornsey, I was rostered first into No 6 Link, which included South London and local goods work. My driver was to be W. Gilbey. Bill also originated from Top Shed and had taken the same decision as me to transfer to Hornsey, although as a driver and after some 25 years as a fireman. Like Joe, Bill had also gained experience on the streamliners. Unusually, for an engineman, Bill's interest was the London theatre, especially first nights, which meant that he preferred day turns. I immediately took a liking to Bill, especially when he allowed me to have the regulator on all the local goods turns. I could see when he fired J6s that his skill with the shovel had not left him. Bill and I built up a useful rapport and eventually we would talk frequently of his exploits at Top Shed.

Some weeks later, I was to learn that Joe Holland had suffered fatal injuries at King's Cross when he was called to answer a phone call from his wife. Apparently, he was walking across the trunking at the north end of the suburban station and was struck down by an oncoming train, a sad memory that still haunts me.

One night whilst enjoying a break at Hither Green, Bill and I got to chatting about his experiences as a Top Link fireman at Top Shed. We dwelt for some time on the streamlined trains. In particular I happened to mention a reference I had seen in O. S. Nock's book *The Locomotives of Sir Nigel Gresley* (page 78) to a run from Newcastle to London with No 2507 *Singapore* in which the driver and fireman were named as Nash and Gilbey respectively. Bill was quite delighted to know that his name had appeared in print, and immediately called this trip to mind, particularly as it was a rarity to have a non-streamlined Pacific on a streamlined train. During one week, A3s were twice used. Although footplate work would have

differed little from that on an A4, the A3 would probably have been flogged within an inch of its life to maintain time but, as chronicled by Mr Nock, both engines gave a good account of themselves. With some satisfaction Bill told me that whilst crossing the Tyne Bridge, just after leaving Newcastle, *Singapore*'s exhaust steam injector failed. Bill's mate instructed him to do his best with the live steam injector, and they would reassess the situation approaching Darlington. After all, they had already lost half an hour or so with the failure of the booked A4, and in any case they could always take the pilot at Darlington if *Singapore* gave them any more trouble. The same situation prevailed as they approached York, and so on, until they arrived at King's Cross, having completed the entire 268 mile journey on one injector, and regaining eight minutes of lost time to boot. What a fascinating trip this must have been!

I like to think that Bill was pleased to have a mate with him who shared his enthusiasm for the job, and it was as a result of one of these footplate chats that he suggested that we arranged to swap turns with a set of men in the main line link for one of their day turns to Peterborough in exchange for one of our night duties to South London. The carrot dangled in front of the main line men was that night duty paid time and a quarter, and often involved a few hours overtime, something that neither of us relished; Bill liked his theatre and I was courting!

I pecked a bit at his suggestion, in view of Joe Holland's somewhat low opinion of my lack of skill with the blade, together with a recent unhappy experience I had had on a trip with another driver on an 'Austerity' 2–8–0 working on Acton via Canonbury duty. Steam was in short supply, and we experienced great difficulty in negotiating the climb from Gospel Oak to Hampstead. I was informed subsequently that I had the misfortune to gain my first 'Austerity' trip with a rogue engine! Apparently, my maximum of 175 psi was as high as anybody else had achieved with this engine, and the driver with whom I was rostered on that occasion had the courtesy to approach me later and apologise, for which I was most grateful. Bill pooh-poohed this self-criticism and offered me encouragement by suggesting that, as a rule, 'Austerities' were good steamers provided one kept the fire thick at the back and thin at the front, and besides he did not think I was that bad with the shovel! He failed to mention, however, that 'Austerities' were extremely rough riders. In the end I agreed to Bill's suggestion.

We arranged to change turns for a 6.05 am turn for 7.30 am ex Ferme Park. The train was No 1090 down mineral empties to New England, rostered for an 'Austerity' 2–8–0. The following Monday morning I signed on. Glancing across to the left of the time sheet, I spotted the number of the engine allotted to us. '60866' – a 'Green Arrow' on my first excursion to Peterborough was something of a shock seeing as I had geared myself to spending the day on an 'Austerity'! I collected a bucket of tools and two bottles of oil from the stores, and made my way out to the shed. There it stood in No 2 road, begrimed, but underneath all that New England filth lurked a V2! The tool situation at Hornsey was less acute than I had experienced at King's Cross and I was glad to be able to spend more time on the engine's preparation. There was a little fire just inside and under the firehole door, and there was sufficient steam and water in the boiler to allow me to proceed. Bill busied himself oiling the engine and carrying out routine examinations. In due course he yelled up to me 'How much steam have you got Bert?' I told him. 'Then move it outside and set it for the middle big end.' I nervously eased the engine out of the shed, and duly set it for oiling the middle big-end (top back angle – near side) as well as leaving it in a position to be able to fill the tank.

Memories of my time as a cleaner at Top Shed came flooding back to me as I made up the back corners of the fire. About $\frac{1}{4}$ ton later, I was able to sweep up, clean the front, and draw a bucket of hot water for us to wash with, preparatory to moving off the shed. With a nice can of freshly made tea in the dish, and a pop on the whistle, Bill at last set 866 in motion.

We arrived at Ferme South Up box and Bill informed the signalman of our train working, and when the board came off we proceeded to use the up spur at Harringay Up Goods under the very bridge where I once sat as a youngster taking engine numbers. For the first time the engine was moving forwards!

The slow climb over Harringay viaduct at last allowed me to enjoy the familiar sound of a Gresley 3-cylinder engine at close quarters. Meanwhile, the large fire that I had prepared at the shed was beginning to burn through slowly. The damper was still closed, and, with minimum blower, small smoky tongues of flame licked from the firehole door; all seemed well and steam pressure was gradually rising.

And so into Ferme Park down side, and straight back on to our train. Our chirpy guard bade us good morning and informed us that we had 60 'private owners' Class A to New England. Had our load been 50 common users we would have been able to run at the faster speed with a 'Green Arrow' in charge. The small shunt signals that bristled in the Down Yard were beginning to come off, the yard shunter's whistle blew and we were ready to leave.

Bill eased the engine away to take up the loose couplings to avoid unnecessary jerking of the train, and with a wave from the guard to indicate that the train was following complete, the engine creaked and grated its way through the complex of track in the Down Yard and out on to the Goods Line, to Wood Green's distant gantry signals just north of Hornsey station. When working a longish train it was prudent to wait at these distants and take advantage of the slightly falling gradient that runs between Hornsey and Wood Green. This gave assistance in getting the train away to a good start, bearing in mind that the single bore tunnel north of Wood Green was on a rising gradient, and, if the train was to travel via the Hertford loop, a running jump at the Bounds Green viaduct.

I now found myself sitting anxiously on the footplate of a 'Green Arrow' reflecting that standing on an engine and wiping the controls in the environs of a shed was a different kettle of fish from actually waiting on an engine for the board to come off. The feeling was somewhat akin to that which one experiences when after sitting for a while in a dentist's waiting room he finally calls you into the surgery! Eventually, the distant came off. No more time for reflections. This was it! My first trip on a Gresley Big Engine.

Open the damper. Spread a little fire from under the door all over the grate and fire to it. By this time, I had about 180 psi on the clock and half a glass of water showing in the boiler. On this occasion, I was shovelling left handed which meant that I was facing Bill. The regulator was

soon fully open. The crescendo of noise was almost deafening as we gathered momentum, with the 3/4 rhythm of the engine and clanking valve gear, together with the odd blow at the front end. I was still shovelling when Bill tapped me on the shoulder. 'That's enough Bert. She's O.K. for the time being.' I looked up at the gauge. The engine was beginning to reach the red mark and to simmer at the valves! On went the exhaust injector. Unlike *Singapore's* this one worked! A glance at the chimney revealed that the soft emission of smoke had a nice cleft in the centre, and the fire had now gone from its original cherry red to almost white. I was able to sit on my seat for a while and enjoy the swaying motion of the engine as we ran through to Wood Green towards the tunnel. Once out of the tunnel, it was necessary to pick up the shovel again, and continue firing in preparation for the tunnel at New Southgate, in so doing helping to keep sulphuric fumes down to a minimum through the second single bore.

At Greenwood we were straight out of the goods line and on to the main; in those days the track was only double to Potters Bar, but, with the tunnels being double-bore, the problem of exhaust inhalation was lessened.

Through the tunnels at Hadley Wood and round the curve at Ganwick 60866 seemed to be enjoying itself, oblivious of the rather secondary train it was hauling. By now I was beginning to enjoy myself as well. As soon as I started to shovel, the engine immediately responded by making steam freely and thus making my initiation into the complexities of firing a wide firebox that much easier.

By the time we emerged from Potters Bar tunnel, Bill was assuming the pose of the driver we had all seen pictures of when working on Gresley locomotives – right hand on the regulator handle high in the roof, and head out of the side window. By now the sound that 60866 was making was quite thrilling, and I feel sure that as we breasted Potters Bar, Bill's Top Link instincts were to give the engine its head, but a loose-coupled train required different skills in its operation from the more glamorous passenger and fitted freight work that a V2 was built for. Moreover, the vacuum brakes on V2s were never the most reliable on loose-coupled trains, as I was to discover on a subsequent trip. It was therefore necessary to ease the engine down and allow the train gently to buffer up with just a whisper of steam at the front end. Nevertheless, we cruised through Hatfield and Welwyn Garden City at a fair clip. We were still main line at Woolmer Green, which allowed Bill to exercise his skills with the water scoop as we ran over the water troughs at Langley, a knack which took me some while to acquire. A blow on the whistle through Stevenage informed the signalman that we would not require water at Hitchin and we were given a run through on the main line.

At last, we were turned slow line at Arlesey and we moved our way along the line until we were brought to a halt at Offord. We took water again as we stood alongside the river Ouse. I later discovered that one never passed a water crane without topping up the tank when working loose-coupled trains. With the welter of traffic on the line at that time, slower trains could be held at the well-known bottlenecks for long periods which made every gallon of water precious. The 'Green Arrows' with 4,200 gallon tenders

were often a problem with water, which was another reason that made them less suitable for slow trains. A large boiler and smallish tender tank could spell trouble!

While we were waiting at Offord, Bill opened the firehole door where he was confronted with what he described as 'a good body of fire'. He suggested that as we moved off, I should make up the back corners and fill a few holes in the rest of the fire and that should get us to Huntingdon.

Here, the shovel was picked up again in readiness for the climb up Stukeley bank to Abbots Ripton, and, with easy steaming down through Connington and over the fens to Yaxley, chimneys and the acrid smell of brickworks told me that the fun was nearly over.

We came to a stand on the Goods Relief road which stood to the west of Peterborough North station where a set of New England men were waiting to relieve us. It was disappointing to have to leave the engine there, rather than take the

train into New England yard and dispose of the engine at the shed as was the normal procedure.

What had started out as a potentially worrying experience for a somewhat nervous teenager developed into what was one of the most pleasant days of his life. There were to be many more trips on Gresley big engines for me, but none seemed ever to capture the magic of that run on 60866. I was never to work on the footplate of this engine again although I often saw it on more prestigious express train working, something that rarely happened to me now that I was ensconced in a principally freight depot.

I later discovered that as Bill was appointed deputy shed foreman at Hornsey, he had arranged with the authorities that if a 'Green Arrow', or similar, should arrive at the shed over the weekend, he would like it kept back for him on the Monday morning – a favour he did me, for which I am eternally grateful.

SELF-CLEANING SMOKEBOXES ON THE V2s

BILL HARVEY

FROM 1940 to 1945 I was employed as Technical Assistant at Gerrards Cross, the wartime Headquarters of the Western Section (GC & GN) of the LNER, Southern Area, dealing with engine casualties, alterations in design and filling temporary vacancies at running sheds created by sickness and holiday relief duties.

Like all Gresley's engines, the V2s were free-steaming and it was not until self-cleaning smokeboxes became general as a result of our experiences with the USA engines, that reports started to come in that the steaming of the V2s had deteriorated.

After Nationalisation, in order to find out what was wrong, a V2 was tested on the plant at Swindon and it was found that whereas the boiler in its original condition could produce 24,000 lb of steam per hour, with the self-cleaning screens in pos-

ition only 14,000 lb was obtainable – a comparatively small alteration to the size and position of the chimney choke, as suggested by Mr S. O. Ell, more than doubled the output *with the screens in position*, viz. 29,000 lb/hour (see BTC Test Bulletin No 8).

The only alteration to firebars that I knew of was made to all classes fitted with drop grates, by the substitution of a multi-bar casting (closely resembling in size and shape a street drain grating) for the individual bars. This was secured by $\frac{1}{2}$ inch countersunk bolts; but these were liable to be displaced by clinker trapped in the hinges, thus preventing the grate from closing, in just the same way that a door with rusted hinges often cannot be closed.

Credit for the modification belongs to Mr Horace Bussey, an old M & GN man, at that time District Boiler Foreman at King's Cross.

Regarding the air spaces, the ratio to grate area in the conventional firebox is usually 50/50. More air can be admitted by making the bars thinner, but these would tend to burn away more quickly due to the fiercer combustion; the usual running shed dodge to overcome any real or fancied deficiency of air was to remove one or two bars and spread the remainder to give a uniform and increased air space.

The French use firebars approximately half the width of those we use, but there are more of them, so the ratio is still around 50/50. They need more and narrower air spaces than we do on account of the nature of their fuel, in order to prevent it from falling straight through and blocking up the ash pan – that really would stop the supply of air to the fire!

V2 class No. 4831 Durham School departing from Nottingham Victoria with a Sunday Cleethorpes to Leicester train on 27th August 1939. With the outbreak of war imminent, the local Territorial standing guard was armed with a rifle but not yet issued with a uniform.

T. G. HEPBURN, RAIL ARCHIVE STEPHENSON

THE 'GREEN ARROW' DERAILMENTS

MICHAEL JOYCE

THE railways of Britain have enjoyed a reputation for being some of the safest in the world but accidents do happen from time to time, and this also applies to specific locomotive types where there are large numbers in a particular class. Under normal conditions, permanent way, locomotives and rolling stock are maintained at a very high level, with steady improvements as new equipment and techniques are evolved, but when a country is fighting a war that lasts six years the situation can change. The demands made on the railway system in Britain during the war years were intense and in the years immediately following there was a huge backlog of work to be done to bring the service back to pre-war standards.

The engines of Class V2 (the 'Green Arrows') came on to the LNER scene in 1936. They were designed for express freight services and, at the outbreak of war in September 1939 there were 76 in service. They had proved to be most successful in carrying out their designed work on express freight services and this had been extended to fast passenger work. At the outbreak of war the railways came under Government control and no more passenger engines could be built. However, because the 'Green Arrows' were designed for freight services initially, the LNER was able to build more of them and, by the end of 1944, there were 184 in service. They handled freight and passenger trains and did sterling work. They had a fine safety record, amassing a total of over 50 million miles without being involved in any serious accident. However, in 1946 this was to change when the V2s were involved in two serious derailments in the Hatfield area, and which resulted in re-examination of two other accidents — one at Newark in 1944 and the other at Thirsk in February 1946.

The accident at Newark took place on 13th March 1944 when an up express of ten coaches, hauled by No 4844, was derailed on straight track when travelling at about 55 mph. The engine, tender and the first five coaches were completely derailed but there was no serious structural damage and no one was injured. The train had just passed over the Muskham water troughs and was approaching the bridge over the river Trent. Later examination showed that there was a single flange mark crossing the cess rail and a series of broken chairs and fishbolts, but no flange marks, for more than 1,000 yards afterwards. The driver thought that neither the engine nor tender was derailed until after they had crossed the bridge, and that the leading coach was derailed beforehand. There was no formal Ministry of Transport inquiry into this accident but the LNER carried out their own. Their conclusions were that a pair of wheels of the leading coach hit an obstruction (a piece of cast iron water scoop was found), and that this resulted in the derailment of the engine, tender and coaches. Although the engine had run approximately 57,000 miles since its last general repair, it was found to be in good condition and it was not considered to be a factor in the accident.

Two years later, on 24th February 1946, another derailment which involved a V2 occurred, this time at Thirsk. No 4878, hauling an up express, was derailed, as was its tender and all ten coaches, but fortunately there were no casualties. Again, the derailment occurred on straight track, which had been renewed a few hours previously but which had not been completely re-ballasted. There was a 20 mph speed restriction in force through the section but the express passed over the new section at 40–50 mph with brakes on. The leading pony truck remained on the track but the leading and driving coupled wheels became derailed after a heavy lurch to the right. After the initial derailment of the driving wheels, the track was burst asunder, and the rest of the train became derailed. Again, there was no official inquiry, but the company inquiry decided that the accident had been caused by excessive speed on practically unballasted track, and that the brakes had probably contributed to the final result, but there was no suggestion that the engine, or any part of its design, was responsible in any

way. Subsequent events, however, brought these two accidents into re-examination and a revision as to their cause.

On Monday, 15th July 1946, the 7.5 pm express passenger train from King's Cross to Aberdeen was approaching Hatfield station on the down main line when it was completely derailed when travelling at about 60 mph. The engine involved was No 3645 and, of the engine and train of fourteen bogie vehicles, only the wheels of the leading pony truck and the rear bogie of the last vehicle (an LMS van) remained on the track. Of the 400 passengers in the train only eleven were injured and detained in hospital.

The engine was built at Darlington in 1942 and had run 184,591 miles since new and 30,177 miles since its last general repair in January 1946. It was normal for V2s to run 70,000 miles between general repairs. At the time of the accident the engine was stabled at Doncaster shed.

The line on the approaches to Hatfield is on a down gradient of 1 in 200 and, at the point of the derailment, takes an easy right-handed curve. At that time there was an overall speed restriction of 60 mph in force south of Hatfield. The track had been re-sleepered and re-chaired from a point 1,126 yards in rear and 174 yards ahead of the point of derailment only 15 days previously. The rails were eight years old and, being only slightly worn, had been used again. The curve had been laid to a cant of $2\frac{3}{4}$ in, which, according to LNER standards, corresponded to a speed of 80 mph for a curve of 76 chains radius. The old ballast had been used again after it had been riddled in dry weather. The gauge was found to be very nearly accurate but there were points where there was some deficiency of ballast, and there had been some evidence of rail creep in the direction of traffic. There had, however, been some reduction in cant from the time the track was relaid and this had become more marked as the point of derailment was reached.

The first sign of derailment was a single light flange mark on the low right-hand rail preceded by some scoring on the running edge of the rail. There was also a sinuous distortion of the track without widening of the gauge. From the flange mark, keys on the low rail were crushed and chairs marked on the outside or broken. There was evidence of a 'carried' wheel for a further 64 yards until a joint in the low rail was released by the fracture of the fishbolts, after which the down main line was completely broken for 235 yards.

Whilst the three leading coaches of the train were wrecked and thrown about over the track, the remaining eleven coaches remained upright. The engine broke away from the train and came to rest upright 112 yards away. The coupled, trailing and tender wheels were derailed to the right but, apart from bruising of the flanges and treads, the engine suffered little damage. The leading pony truck remained on the rails.

The engine was being handled by Driver M. Hudson and Fireman G.W. Lancaster of Grantham shed who had worked V2s for over four years on main line expresses. Driver Hudson stated that 3645 was in very good condition and had been running steadily until just after the Red Hall signal box. There was a heavy roll, or lurch, to the left which was much more violent than the slight rolling normally experienced on that curve with a fast train. The engine did not roll back to the right as would have been expected, and a few seconds later there was violent vibration which indicated that the engine had been derailed. He applied the brakes and then realised that the engine had parted from the train but that there was no 'backward snatch' at any time, which indicated to him that the engine became derailed before the tender, and the tender before the train.

The engine had been examined in a 'light tunnel' at Peterborough the previous day and was found to be in good condition. Drivers who had worked the engine the previous day also gave satisfactory reports. After the accident 3645 was taken to Doncaster works and completely stripped and examined.

Apart from the damage previously mentioned, which was minor in character, some brake work was bent and twisted, and the tender main frames strained and some axle boxes broken, but all this was due to the derailment. The tyres and flanges were of satisfactory profile; the axles were true and there had been no binding in the horns. There was, however, considerable wear of the pony swing links but, as the links were always under load,

it was considered that it would not have affected the side control action. Two of four coil springs of the pony axle were found to be broken (one on each side). The fractures were of long standing and the springs had closed up slightly and carried their loads. It was reported that such fractures were not unusual. The engine and tender were weighed and, apart from the two broken springs, appeared to be in normal condition considering the mileage run since last general repairs. There was some increase in side play of the engine axle boxes and the pony truck, but this was not thought to be excessive.

The Inspecting Officer (Lt Col G. R. S. Wilson) talked with a number of drivers and permanent way inspectors and all were of the opinion that there was no great difference in the riding characteristics between the V2s and the Pacifics, but, if anything, the V2s were more inclined to sideways nosing movements and the Pacifics to rolling. He later made two footplate journeys between King's Cross and Grantham on a V2 (909) and then on an A1 (later A3) No 104. On good track there was little difference between the two types up to speeds of 70 mph (the maximum at that time), but he felt that the V2 was rather more sensitive to local track irregularities, and that there was continuous rolling and nosing between Hornsey and Wood Green at speeds between 45 and 50 mph. He found that, when a roll to the left occurred, it coincided with a sideways movement of the front of the engine to the right, and vice versa.

After the detailed examinations had been concluded, and taking into account his conversations and personal footplate experiences, Lt Col Wilson came to the conclusion that this derailment had been due to the leading coupled wheels breaking two bolts of a short fishplate, thus releasing a joint of the low rail, and the track was subsequently demolished. Whilst the wheels of the pony truck were not derailed, he felt the two broken coil springs had no bearing on the course of events, but, because of the arrangement of the swing link pony axle, there would be little or no damping friction, and that an undue proportion of the guiding force would be developed at the flanges of the leading coupled wheels. Under such circumstances, if the track were weak laterally, a high flange pressure would result in its distortion. This being so, it was felt

that the underlying cause was the heavy roll to the outside of the curve which brought some relief of weight on the inside coupled wheel and that its flange was exercising a high lateral pressure which would cause it to mount the rail.

As a direct result of these conclusions, the derailments at Newark and Thirsk, where V2s were also involved, were reconsidered, and a view expressed that the causes were probably the same as at Hatfield – interaction between the locomotives and track at comparatively high speeds. Lt Col Wilson made a recommendation that consideration might be given to an improvement of the front end side control on the V2s.

Four months later, on 10th November 1946, another serious derailment occurred, at Marshmoor, just south of Hatfield, and again a 'Green Arrow' was involved.

The 4.45 pm express from Newcastle to King's Cross, which comprised twelve bogie vehicles and was hauled by No 905 (originally 4876), became completely derailed on the up main line when travelling at about 55 mph when entering an easy right-handed curve 400 yards south of the Marshmoor signal box. The engine and the twelve coaches remained in a fair line except for the fourth which was overturned, and the fifth which was partially overturned. There was little damage to the bodies of the coaches, but the bogies and undergear were damaged. Apart from its brake rigging, the engine was practically undamaged. Fortunately the train was lightly loaded and only seven passengers complained of minor injuries or shock.

The engine was stabled at King's Cross and, by pure coincidence, had been in an accident at Potters Bar in February 1946 but, on that occasion, it had been hauling a down express which ran into the wreckage of a local train that had run into the buffer stop on the up slow line. No 905 was built at Darlington in 1940 and had run 390,864 miles since new, and 49,625 miles since its last general repair in December 1945. There was no evidence of any material defects in the engine prior to the accident and, apart from the brake work and bruising of the treads and flanges of the derailed wheels, it was virtually undamaged.

The initial derailment was to the inside of a long right-handed curve of 92 chains radius, approximately 130 yards beyond its commencing tangent point, and 40 yards beyond the end of the transition. The up main line had been re-sleepered and re-chaired in July 1946 from a point 1,072 yards to the rear to 33 yards ahead of the point of derailment. The 100 lb RBS rails, which showed little signs of wear, had been replaced on that occasion. The curve was aligned to pegs which had been put in by a fresh survey in April 1946 with a transition length of 90 yards with the cant running from zero at the tangent point to the designed figure of 2 in for the circular curve. This would correspond to a speed of approximately 85 mph on a curve of 93 chains radius.

There had been a long-standing problem of drainage at this point and the ballast was a mixture of flint and slag. It was somewhat dirty and had been cleared from the ends of some sleepers to drain the water out. Comprehensive draining work had been carried out at the site on the day of the accident, and on the three previous Sundays. Some work had been done on the down main line, resulting in a 20 mph speed restriction, but there was only the normal 60 mph restriction in force on the up main line. However, this track was due for work similar to that on the down main after that had been completed.

After the derailment, the gauge and superelevation of the up main line were measured and tested using void-meters. It was discovered that there were marked irregularities in cant through the transition to the point of derailment, and that these variations were mainly on the high rail.

The first sign of a derailment was a deep flange mark on a chair key of the right-hand (low) rail, followed at a short distance further on by broken chairs under both rails. There were no flange marks on either rail but there was a streak of black grease four yards long on the running edge of the high rail some 21 yards in the rear of the first mark. There was also a sinuous distortion of the track, without appreciable widening of gauge, about 54 yards to the rear of the grease mark, and 75 yards to the rear of the first marked key. This distortion was very similar to that found at the derailment at Hatfield in July 1946. As the wheels of the pony truck remained on the track, they held the engine to within a foot or so of track alignment, and this, with the effect of the Buckeye couplings, kept the train more or less in line and prevented a much more serious accident.

The engine had come on to the train at Grantham and was being handled by Driver E. J. Hills and Fireman C. E. Brooks

of King's Cross shed. It left Grantham 12 minutes late and further time was lost due to signal checks, and Huntingdon was passed 24 minutes late. Afterwards it had a clear run and had regained two minutes on passing Hatfield. Driver Hills reported that the engine was in good condition and he had no difficulty in keeping time with the moderate load. At Hatfield the engine was running freely at 10% cut-off and the regulator barely open. At the Hatfield No 2 box he experienced severe rolling and he shut off steam. He was about to apply the brakes when the engine steadied. He then coasted for about $\frac{1}{4}$ mile and then opened the regulator to the first valve in order to get over the rising 1 in 200 gradient to Potters Bar. He estimated that he was travelling at about 50 mph (or a little more) through the overbridge at Marshmoor. The engine then gave a sudden heavy lurch to the right and was derailed almost at once. The signalman at Marshmoor box expressed an opinion that the train was travelling at 70 mph when it passed, but the Inspecting Officer (Lt Col G. R. S. Wilson) preferred to accept the view given by Driver Hills when the booked times, the gradient and the check at Hatfield were taken into account.

Driver Hills made the point that it was well known for many years that rough riding could be expected on both main lines at Marshmoor, and reports of lurches had been received from time to time. On every occasion these reports were checked and the track examined and corrected if necessary. Sometimes, following a report, the Marshmoor distant signal would be kept at caution pending track examination. The last time that this had been done was on 30th August, but no reports had been received for two months preceding this derailment.

Lt Col Wilson took statements from the drivers of five other trains using the up main line during the hours preceding the derailment and their comments are interesting.

7.45 pm	A3	55–60 mph	'I felt a violent lurch'
8.02 pm	V2	45–50 mph	'We felt nothing serious'
8.55 pm	V2	50–55 mph	'We got a lurch and a roll'
9.21 pm	A4	45–50 mph	'We got a bit of a kick which was not too serious'
10.20 pm	V2	40 mph	'I felt three successive lurches in the first 100 yards from the bridge when travelling at 40 mph'
10.35 pm	V2	55 mph	Train derailed.

Following the accident, the engine was taken to Doncaster Works and given a thorough examination. The axles were found to be true and there had been no binding in the horns. There was appreciable wear in the bushes of the pony swing

links, but, as these are always under load, the side control was not affected. The side play in all the axles of the engine was checked and was considered not to be excessive. One of the four coil springs of the pony axle was found to have been broken for some time but had still been carrying its load. After weighing the engine it was found that there was approximately one ton less than standard on the pony truck and one ton more than standard on the leading coupled axle.

Apart from the broken spring, the engine appeared to be in normal condition with regard to the mileage run since its last overhaul.

Permanent way staffs were closely questioned on the problems met in the Marshmoor area, and the work that had to be done on a regular basis. It was, therefore, recognised that there *were* unsatisfactory conditions and that these had not been helped by shortage of labour due to the war.

Lt Col Wilson, in his summing up, had no hesitation in accepting that the up main track had been left in a satisfactory condition as regards alignment and cross level when a gang had completed their day's work at 4.30 pm on the day of the accident. However, that condition was not maintained under conditions of traffic and, by 10.20 pm, there was practically no margin of safety at any higher speed than 40 mph. He concluded that, as the irregularity of the cross level was of a different order from the comparatively minor variations at Hatfield in July 1946, it was the primary cause of the derailment.

He went on to comment that there were features of this derailment that bore a marked resemblance to the previous derailments at Hatfield, Newark and Thirsk, namely preliminary track distortion and the fact that the leading pony truck, in all cases, had not been derailed. He suggested that the engines of Class V2 were more than ordinarily sensitive to track defects. He repeated his recommendation that attention might be given to changes in the redesign of the pony truck.

When the Ministry of Transport are involved in an inquiry into an accident the recommendations of the Inspecting

Officer carry a great deal of weight. They are not mandatory, but where the safety of the public is involved, it would be foolish for them to be ignored. Lt Col Wilson showed considerable understanding of the situation facing the LNER at that time (1946) when the company was confronted by very serious problems as a result of the war. They were trying to deal with a huge backlog of locomotive overhauls and permanent way work, and to improve the railway services. Because the swing link pony truck in the V2s was sensitive to track variations, it posed a potential risk. There were those, as always, who were ready to make suggestions that the engines were dangerous.

The Inspecting Officer could have recommended that the V2s be withdrawn from service until the modifications had been carried out or that they be used only on slow, or medium speed, freight trains. This would have placed the LNER in a most difficult situation for they relied on the V2s to take a considerable part in working passenger trains until the Pacifics were all back to normal condition. However, Lt Col Wilson suggested that the problem should be dealt with by having

a more rigorous policy of local speed restrictions, particularly at those places which were recognised as being most troublesome. This was a very sound recommendation and, whilst it would mean some delays for a period, it did allow the LNER to maintain its passenger services.

Following the accidents, and the subsequent recommendations, the LNER started to change the design of the pony trucks on the V2s using the spring side control type as fitted to the 2–6–4T Class L1.

The first V2 to have the conversion was No 884 (originally 4855) and this was in service within four weeks of the Marshmoor derailment. A further 25 were ordered in November 1946, and in June 1947 authority was given to convert the remaining 158 engines and, to the end of their days, there were no further accidents involving the V2s that could be attributed to the design of the pony truck.

It is, perhaps, interesting to contemplate whether these derailments (and the consequent need to make modifications) would have occurred had it not been for the war which placed abnormal demands on both locomotives and

permanent way. Under normal peace-time conditions the track would have been maintained to high standards, and improvements made from time to time. The swing link truck had been used for many years in the K3 2–6–0s, which were used on express freight trains and, to a limited degree, on passenger trains, without any serious problems. It was well known that the K3s could be rough at times, but this was something that was accepted by enginemen. All engine types had their characteristics but there had never been any serious concern expressed by the men who regularly handled the 'Green Arrows', and it is reasonable to assume that there would have been if they had thought that they were dangerous in any way.

The author has drawn heavily on the Ministry of Transport Accident Reports, listed below, in the writing of this article, and would like to express appreciation to H.M. Stationery Office for having granted permission to use, and quote from, the Reports.

References:
Ministry of Transport Accident Reports
Hatfield – 15th July, 1946
Marshmoor – 10th November, 1946

V2 No. 60911 hauling the King's Cross to Niddrie goods, between the Welwyn tunnels, in 1953.

G. W. GOSLIN

LNER MANAGERS HAVE THEIR SAY

SIR NIGEL GRESLEY – A PERSONAL RECOLLECTION

J. F. HARRISON O.B.E.

WHEN one of your Vice Presidents asked me to say a few words about Sir Nigel Gresley in your 25th Anniversary year, on the grounds that I was probably his oldest premium apprentice or pupil still alive, I felt very honoured, but most inclined to say 'no' because during the years that Sir Nigel occupied the post of CME of the LNER, I was on the GC Section, far away from the centre of things on the Main Line, and therefore my recollections were few and far between. However, as I have always been a fan of Sir Nigel, I felt I should try and say something of interest. You are fortunate to have such excellent articles by Norman Newsome upon carriage and wagon matters, so I do not propose to enlarge on them, but rather confine my remarks to incidents and to design matters up to 1923.

My first meeting with Mr Gresley, as he then was, took place in his office at Doncaster, when I went to be interviewed to see if I was suitable for a position as a premium apprentice. Apparently I was, for on 1st February 1921 I started in the top turnery at the Plant Works. I mention this shop, because I have only recently found a letter by Mr Gresley to my mother, saying the foreman under whom I served my trial month had reported I was satisfactory, therefore he, Mr Gresley, would be pleased to accept me as a premium apprentice. I never knew that our future career depended upon the foreman of the top turnery, who was called Treece and installed discipline into his lads by unexpectedly giving them a kick on the backside!

After three years' apprenticeship I asked Mr Gresley if I could become a pupil of his, because pupilage enabled me to have training in pattern shop, foundry, carriage work and drawing office – none of which was covered in the premium apprentice curriculum. This was agreed and in due time, on completion, I went to the Loco Running Department at Doncaster, and from there to the Southern Area HQ at Liverpool Street, my job being to investigate locomotive failures. Often when I got back into King's Cross I used

to go to the messengers' office to have a cup of tea. These messengers were very grand in their uniforms. One day the head one said 'Why don't you go and see Mr Gresley?' I said 'I've nothing to say to him'. However, out he went, and said 'Mr G. will see you now.' Imagine my panic! However, there was nothing for it but to go in. He asked me how I was getting on, and what I was doing, and then said 'Would you like to go back into the Works? I have a vacancy for Assistant to the Works Manager at Gorton.' I jumped at the idea and he then asked me what my salary was. I told him £325 per annum. 'We'll make it £425, just wait a moment whilst I confirm it with Mr Bell.' He came back and said 'Mr Bell says you can only have a rise of £50 because you had a rise of £25 a little over a year ago.' This illustrates how great a part luck plays in one's life, as Gresley had intended to settle the job that weekend and I was only third on the list! This also shows how tight money was, not only for salaries but also all new works, experiments, and so on – just the things that H.N.G. needed money for. It makes one wonder what he would have achieved given the sort of money that was poured into the 'tilting train'.

Sir Nigel came to Gorton a number of times whenever there was something to interest him, such as new monobloc castings for three-cylinder locomotives, certain war work, and new schemes for renewing machine tools. In these visits he took an interest in the Caprotti valved four-cylinder 4–6–0s, which were not particularly good economically, but did provide an alternative form of valve operation, and I think this set his mind to thinking on these lines, hence the D49 with Lentz gear.

On one visit, he asked me if I would drive him to the Midland Hotel. I had at that time a 2-litre MG which was fitted with hydraulic jacks to each wheel, operated by a pump and distributor valve, situated under the passenger's seat. Of all things, I had a puncture, and had to ask him to get out whilst I did the necessary. He was so fascinated by the idea that he said would I go over to Doncaster, explain

the system to the Chief Draughtsman and get him to draw up a similar scheme for the J52 shunters, which were always being derailed. The idea came to nothing for obvious reasons, but it illustrates his interest in anything that could be applied to rolling stock.

On another occasion he looked over a scheme for replacing all the machine tools in the machine and wheel shop. He agreed and said 'I want every scheme vetted by the accountant and showing a saving of not less than 10%.' When I told him that a single operator, say a piston rod grinder, could not be dispensed with as we only wanted one off – 'Oh well, you won't have a new one then' – the result was that by a great deal of wangling we got our unit machines. This asking for what he knew could not be achieved meant that he got the best possible solution – a very similar approach to Dr Beeching's.

One occasion at Doncaster is worth a mention. He went into the paint shop, up into the cab of a Pacific and said 'Give me a piece of paper'. On it he sketched a device of levers for the water gauge cocks so that both cocks were closed simultaneously if a glass burst, without the driver getting scalded (there had been such an accident a day or two before) – an immediate solution which became standard. He personally was concerned with details when they became important, not when they were just ordinary run-of-the-mill stuff.

I have mentioned one or two moments I can remember that illustrate his enormous interest in new ideas and his awareness of the place of the main workshops. It has often been said that he did not take much interest in the equipment at locomotive sheds. I think the phenomenal shortage of money meant that what little could be spared for maintenance of rolling stock had to be channelled into the main workshops where a saving could be obtained, whereas a number of machine tools in sheds were infrequently used, only being needed in emergencies.

Sir Nigel's early years are well known. In 1903 he was appointed C & W Superintendent at Doncaster at the age of 27, and eight years later he became Loco-motive Superintendent of the Great Northern Railway. It was clear the Direc-tors had great confidence in this young man.

When he took over from H. A. Ivatt in 1911, the GNR was very short of freight engines, so for the next ten years, through the war, he concentrated on this particular need without giving much thought to main line passenger locomotives. I have no doubt that had the war not occurred, this ten-year-period would have been much reduced; perhaps the GN would have had a Pacific in 1920.

Like other CMEs settling into this enor-mous job, he perpetuated the designs of his predecessor, such as the J6 0–6–0s, quite good engines but small-wheeled at 5 ft 2 in and therefore limited in speed.

To increase speed potential it would be necessary to increase the wheel diameter to at least 5 ft 8 in, and, on looking around, he noted that the GW had built a 2–6–0 with 5 ft 8 in diameter wheels, the 4300 class, which was most successful. So he produced his first locomotive design, intended to meet the GN needs for a good, reliable, fast freight engine, the first K1, No 1630, with 5 ft 8 in wheels, 20 in × 26 in cylinders, and 10 in piston valves in outside steam chests. The Walschaerts valve gear had a Gresley modification, a guide to carry a small crosshead to take the weight of the combination lever, which became standard. On the other hand,

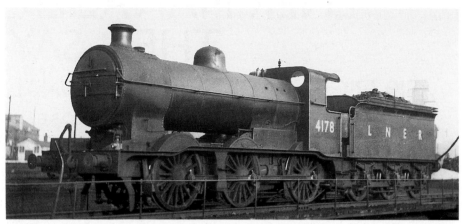
J6 class No. 4178 (originally No. 3529) at Grantham c.1947. This was one of the earlier members of the class, with the boiler set forward, longer cab, and inside sandboxes.   JOHN F. CLAY

In this 1913 photograph, one of H. N. Gresley's original 2–6–0 design, GNR H2 class (LNER K1) No. 1635, looks in pristine condition, hauling a fast goods train of ventilated vans.   LCGB

Gresley's first 2–8–0 was classified O1 by both the Great Northern and the LNER. In this view No. 470 appears to be running on the fast line with a train of coal empties. The combination of a Gresley engine coupled to a Stirling tender was not usual.   COLLECTION A. B. COLLINS

piston tail rods did not become standard.

In December 1913 came the first 2–8–0, a two-cylinder enlarged version of the K1 concept, which was capable of working 80 coal wagons on the Peterborough to Hornsey run, an increase in train loading of 30% compared with Ivatt's 'Long Toms', 0–8–0s. These 2–8–0s were the first with outside steam pipes, and boilers of similar size to the Atlantics. These engines had 21 in × 28 in cylinders and were consequently over-cylindered. Gresley drew the conclusion that, given the large diameter boiler, 20 in × 26 in cylinders seemed to give the right balance in future.

In 1914 the K1 was fitted with a larger 5 ft 6 in boiler and became the ubiquitous K2, which could also be said to be the model for Thompson's B1. I remember driving a K2, hauling 17 coaches from King's Cross to York during the General Strike and, worst of all, stopping at all stations, which meant at smaller places drawing up twice and occasionally three times. The three times was probably due to my bad stopping in the first place, but you can imagine how long the journey took, something like nine hours!

Except for some 0–6–0s, this brought to an end new construction during the war years as Doncaster and other works were turned over to war work, but one very important event took place which influenced Gresley immensely, and that was the rebuilding of No 3279 into a four-cylinder Atlantic. To cut a long story short, this four-cylinder locomotive was not a success, so much so that Gresley never considered four-cylinder simple expansion for the rest of his career. He scrapped the original proposal for a Pacific design of a four-cylinder parallel-boilered one. To me this seemed a basic change in thought, and a good one.

So towards the end of the war, the first three-cylinder locomotive with conjugated valve gear was built, 2–8–0 No 461. Trials of this engine satisfied Gresley that he was on a winner and from then on his mind was firmly fixed on three cylinders, large boilers and his own conjugated valve gear. Superheating was an additional means of improving the performance of all locomotives, and although he invented his own type of double header superheater, he eventually accepted and standardised the Robinson single-header superheater.

After the war, the GNR was still short of freight engines and so he designed an

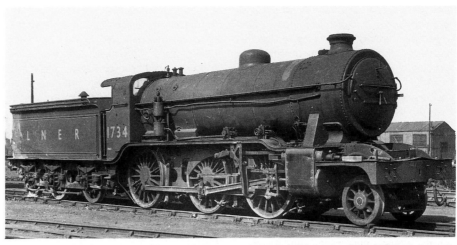

One of the GNR's mixed traffic workhorses, renumbered 1734 in the 1946 LNER series and transferred to the Great Eastern section, is seen here at Stratford in 1947 in rather grubby lined green livery.
RAS MARKETING (PHOTOMATIC)

This 2–8–0, No. 3461, was Gresley's first 3-cylinder locomotive, with his original form of derived valve motion for the inside cylinder. It is seen here with an up coal train, emerging from Hadley Wood South tunnel. The distinctive slope of the outside cylinders is particularly apparent here.
RAS MARKETING (PHOTOMATIC)

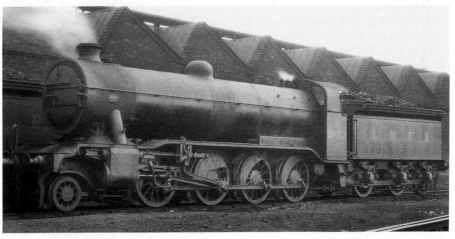

O2 class No. 3493 was one of a batch ordered on Doncaster by the Great Northern, but not delivered until after the LNER had been formed. The shorter chimney conformed to the group composite load gauge. This loco and its companions worked coal trains between New England and Ferme Park for over twenty years.
RAS MARKETING (PHOTOMATIC)

enlarged K2, namely the K3 with three cylinders and a 6 ft diameter boiler. This large boiler was the next step forward in his Pacific thinking. Nickel-chrome rods were used for the first time as a spin-off from the Pennsylvania K4s class, which had always been in his mind. It should be noted that the K3s had long-travel valves six years before the interchange trials, with 1 $\frac{1}{2}$ in lap and 6$\frac{3}{8}$ in travel in full gear of 75%. So much for the idea that H.N.G. had not considered long-travel valves before the interchange trials! I can still remember those engines from their rough riding, which was quite something. Again Gresley must have heard comments on this aspect, which would encourage him to have carrier wheels if possible.

However, by 1920/21 his mind was firmly fixed on a three cylinder Pacific design and it is noticeable that when the specification for 1470 was drawn up, it bore a remarkable resemblance to a reduced K4s Pacific of the Pennsylvania Railroad, which engine had been evolved after years of testing on their test plant at Altoona and had a wide firebox, large tapered boiler with combustion space, was superheated, had his own conjugated valve gear and the knowledge that plenty of steam could be supplied to meet all conditions. This locomotive, which appeared in April 1922, was known as 1470 *Great Northern*. After minor alterations it became the prototype for the world's steam engine record for speed and all the load-carrying high speed record firsts. These included the non-stop London–Edinburgh run of 393 miles, and such load-hauling records as 850 tons from Peterborough to King's Cross by 2549. One of the alterations that appeared was, of course, long-travel valves. Another was an increase in boiler pressure to 220 lb per sq in and then streamlining.

This brief reference to the gradual improvements made, covers the period up to the A4s and their super trains. The 'Silver Jubilee', 'Coronation' and 'West Riding' all added immensely to the great man's success, who was now acknowledged as one of the great locomotive engineers of the world. It may be worth mentioning that a proposed design for a 4–8–2 locomotive was being considered at the time of World War II. It was in fact an enlarged Pacific with no unique features, merely a continuation of the Gresley theme.

As usual with great men, there are always critics for one reason or another,

and his critics naturally focused on his conjugated valve gear, middle big end failures and hot axleboxes. Some of us were equally aware of the need to find solutions to these undoubted problems and it was not until after Sir Nigel's untimely early death in 1941, and the interim period

under Edward Thompson, that these matters could be tackled under Arthur Peppercorn's guidance.

He decided, urged by E. Windle and myself, to build a Pacific which would reflect Sir Nigel's ideas and bring into practice solutions covering the criticisms made, namely a locomotive with three separate valve gears and roller bearing

axleboxes. These locomotives became known as the Peppercorn A1s. Because of the reduction in failures due to hot bearings and longer periods between shoppings, they achieved mileages of 120,000 between heavy repairs, considerably better than any other of the constituent companies' engines. They gave figures such as these: 228 miles per calendar day per locomotive; 4.5% under and awaiting repair in the shops; and 9.5% under and awaiting shed repair.

Peppercorn would have been the first person to acknowledge that his Pacifics were in fact what we were all certain would have been Gresley's. I may say that these engines were individually costed under BR (LMR engine costing) against Kings, Castles, Duchesses and Merchant Navies and, much to the chagrin of the LMS heirarchy at 222 Marylebone Road, they came out substantially cheaper than all the others, in spite of the fact that no account was taken of the increased track maintenance of the LMR due to con-

tinuous blow down. Individual costing ceased forthwith!

On nationalisation, the Mechanical Engineering Dept. was completely dominated by LMS people. Somewhat naturally, they pushed their ideas on standardisation very hard, with the result that apart from some Gresley features, the basic designs were LMS and I felt we would never be able to continue Gresley's successful designs at all, until it was decided to design the BR Class 8 Pacific at Derby. So C. S. Cocks, ex-LNER via Bulleid and the Southern, who was Chief Draughtsman, was equally determined with me that we would

The K3 2—6—0s were in demand in most parts of the LNER system, when excursion trains were being worked. This picture shows No. 1164 at Nottingham Victoria with an up train formed of green and cream tourist stock.
T. G. HEPBURN RAIL ARCHIVE STEPHENSON

A New England-based K3, No. 61864 leaving Welwyn South tunnel in June 1958. The leading two coaches were a Gresley steel-sided articulated set,

G. W. GOSLIN

produce a locomotive with as much Gresley as possible. We managed to get the rotary cam gear boxes of Caprotti design (thus avoiding any question of derived valve gear), a new forked end middle big end (thus avoiding hot middle big ends), roller bearing axleboxes (no hot bearings), new type carrier boxes replacing Cartazzi and giving a good ride, plus already standardised Gresley parts such as three-bar crossheads and new piston lubrication arrangements to reduce piston ring wear. The greatest care was taken to ensure streamlined steam passageways. I had been impressed by the need for this streamlining after examining the LM Duchesses which suffered from loose cylinders, and where connections between the outside cylinders, frame plates and inside cylinders were like a minor staircase. This streamlining undoubtedly helped 71000 to give 15.7% thermal efficiency, representing 86% of what is theoretically possible, and a steam consumption of 12.2 lbs per IHP

hour, the lowest figure recorded by any steam locomotive, due to the Caprotti rotary cam gear and streamlined passageways.

So I think it fair to say that Gresley's influence lasted right to the end of the steam era, and I am only too happy to say that those design features of No 71000 which we incorporated were basic Gresley thinking, improvements perhaps on his world beaters, but nevertheless improvements I am sure he would have carried out had he been in charge when 71000 was designed.

All Sir Nigel's achievements were created against a background of extreme financial stringency and this makes them all the more meritorious. Before Locomotive Committee meetings there was always a meeting of the Chairman, Andrew K. McCosh and the CME, and it was always 'Can't you do with less in number?' or 'Can we reduce the cost by buying abroad?' — anything to reduce the demand for money.

I believe that when Nationalisation came, the LNER would have been bankrupt in another six to nine months.

Sir Nigel's great success generated and encouraged a great *esprit de corps* among all the staff from top to bottom, which certainly did not exist in BR days, nor does it appear to rear its head today to any noticeable extent.

What little I have said about Sir Nigel and his achievements in no way lessens the enormous admiration I had for him, nor in any way alters my personal view that along with Chapelon they were the two outstanding locomotive engineers of all time. I finish with a quotation Sir George Porter made at a Dimbleby Lecture on 'Knowledge itself is power', that while Faraday and Watt gave freedom and happiness to far more people than Abraham Lincoln, it was the pursuit of knowledge that made Sir Nigel Gresley outstanding.

With only three years of a distinguished career remaining, A3 class No. 60055 Woolwinder *is shown here fitted with a double blastpipe and chimney.*
GRESLEY SOCIETY COLLECTION

One of the original ten K3s built for the Great Northern, No. 4005, by this time fitted with an early group standard 4,200 gallon tender, approaching York from the south on 21st August 1937. The train was probably bound for Scarborough, and the loco would have been changed at York.

H. C. DOYLE

SALAD DAYS IN STEAM

TERRY MILLER

IT had always been an acknowledged fact that apprenticeship in a railway works provided a thoroughly sound training in mechanical engineering, but in the years between the two world wars the companies took on a rather greater number of apprentices than they could eventually absorb in regular adult employment. This was not intended to be a means of employing juvenile labour in order to save money, although the companies might have been forgiven for doing so during the slump years of the late twenties and early thirties. What then was the purpose?

The answer was simple – and honourable. In those years there were many railways overseas that looked to this country to provide them with almost all the trained railway engineers they needed and many young men from railway workshops soon made their way overseas when they were 'out of their time'. Of course it was only to be expected that the UK railways themselves would retain a proportion of their trainees and they made it their business to keep a fairly close eye on their apprentices and to be selective when it came to meeting their own requirements.

Thus it was that early in his last year of apprenticeship in an LNER main works, a premium apprentice might expect to be called upon to experience a frightening ordeal. He was required to appear before the Apprentices' Training Committee, the membership of which consisted of a Mechanical Engineer and the Locomotive Running Superintendent of each of the Areas into which the LNER was divided at that time. The Assistant Chief General Manager of the LNER, Robert Bell, was the Chairman. Before that august assembly of senior railway officers the unfortunate apprentice sat alone on the opposite side of a huge boardroom table and was required to give account of himself. The Area Mechanical Engineer under whom, until then, he had served his time, was briefed to speak concerning his protégé's attributes and his failings, if he had any, and his attainments in the technical college he had attended on day-release. And finally he was asked about his aspirations and, if the Committee had been duly impressed, whether he would like to spend six months of the remaining period of his

A grimy K2, No. 61670, approaching Grimsby Town station with a Cleethorpes holiday excursion in the 1930s.
JOHN F. CLAY

apprenticeship in the Locomotive Running Department.

This question was, as the reader will readily believe, usually answered in the affirmative and a week or two later the young man was transferred to one of the large running sheds, there to spend four months as a fitter and two months on the footplates of locomotives in service.

At one time apprentices were employed as firemen whilst gaining their footplate experience but by 1932 this practice had been discontinued and we rode as third man. That, however, did not mean we did not fire engines; the regular firemen were usually not unwilling to hand over the shovel.

Having done my four months as a fitter at Doncaster Carr Sheds, I was told to report to Inspector Slaughter, a large and weighty gentleman who told me to go and ride on the engine working No 2 Pilot in the hump yard. It was an ex-GCR 2–8–0 No 5399 working empty wagons into Hexthorpe 'gulley' and loaded coal wagons thence to the mineral bank.

Somehow Inspector Slaughter's demeanour, though pleasant, had left me with the impression that he did not require me to ask him daily what I was to do if,

indeed, I asked him at all. So I thenceforth arranged my own timetable, booking on and off as I chose. Thus I promoted myself through the links, fairly rapidly – firstly Lincoln pick-up goods, then coal from Bullcroft to Wakefield, followed by express coal to Peterborough and finished my first week with a passenger train to York, a fast from there to Hull and fish back to Doncaster. This day's work was with a K2 2–6–0 No 4658. The high spot from York to Hull was the fast run down through Beverley; on the 7 miles of 1 in 155 (average) falling gradient, progress of the old Ragtimer was neither silent nor smooth running. The almost flat cab roof flapped up and down what looked to be a good foot! It was not very difficult to realise the reason for locomotives of this class being known as Ragtimers.

It struck me as a good idea to acquaint myself with locomotive work in as many different types of service as I could cover in the time available. So coal trains, pick-up freights and stopping passenger trains occupied a week or more, though I admit finding it possible to fit in another couple of trips on the 10.05 am York to Hull; the run down through Beverley on a K2 was too good to miss!

Semi-fast passenger trains came next, taking me to Peterborough, Lincoln, Boston, Skegness and March on a variety of engines of different types but including an introduction to Atlantics and Pacifics.

The real thrills began when trips to King's Cross and back came on the list – and with that, introduction to some of the top link drivers. As far as possible these men had their regular engines and the incentive to good time-keeping that this provided was quite remarkable. Under all circumstances main line drivers did their utmost to keep good time in those days; it was almost a religion and woe betide any guard who entered on his daily ticket any delay allegedly due to loss of time by the locomotive which was not accepted by the driver. There was never much love lost between drivers and guards and an altercation about loss of time could lead to some pretty fiery words. I daresay that the change from steam to diesel and electric traction has not greatly changed this time-honoured feature of railway operation.

Trips to King's Cross and back were most enjoyable but meant hard work too. Firing a Pacific with a load of 450 tons or more over 156 miles or even 312 miles was a real challenge. Whilst the regular fireman could not be expected to be reluctant to hand over his shovel, even to a novice, the attitude of the drivers was a commendable readiness to let you have a go. Not to the extent of causing any loss of time by falling pressure, of course, but showing tolerance of occasional shovelfuls missing the firehole altogether, especially if the riding of the engine was not always silky smooth as, indeed, it seldom was.

Firing a Pacific with its wide firebox required the fireman to master special skill in handling the shovel in order to keep sufficient coal in the back corners of the grate. That spot could not be reached by a direct throw from the blade of the shovel; instead the shovel had to be inserted through the firehole and then swung so that the shaft of the shovel pivoted against the horizontal centre of the firehole opposite to the corner into which the coal was to be deposited. In the same movement the shovel had to be turned over a quarter of a turn so that the coal flew off the blade cleanly in the desired direction. Once learned, the knack was not difficult; the only trying feature was the effect on the right hand (if you were right-handed) of the split-second that the movement occupied and during which the

same hand was exposed to the glare of the white-hot fire in the firebox. The use of a rag to wrap round the hand or even the wearing of a glove was not uncommon but seemed to carry a slight stigma of being rather less than professional.

Regular firemen on Pacifics mastered the art quite readily, having graduated on Atlantics with their wide fireboxes. The V2 class 2–6–2 had not, by 1932, come into existence.

There was a temptation, once having experienced trips on the main line, to continue with them rather than seek to learn what went on in the way of less glamorous work, but being now in the second month of my time on the footplate, I changed to something involving less mileage but no less interesting.

Engine No 3271 was one on which I had done a few repair jobs whilst on fitting work in the shed. Almost exactly 30 years

No. 2746 Fairway *heading an up Leeds train, passing No. 2595* Trigo *on the down 'Flying Scotsman' at Grantham in August 1936, before the A4s appeared in quantity.* JOHN F. CLAY

old, 3271 began life as a 4-cylinder 'small' 4–4–2 in 1902 and was unique in that although it had four cylinders, it had only two valve spindles. Each of these carried four valve heads, the port openings for the outside cylinders being controlled by the two inner heads on each spindle and the inside cylinders by the outer heads. This arrangement was not satisfactory so balanced slide valves were fitted in 1904. Those for the inside cylinders were actu-

ated by Stephenson link motion and those for the outside cylinders by Walschaerts gear. Still considered to be unsatisfactory, the engine was rebuilt in 1911 with two inside cylinders only and in this form ran on until scrapped in 1936. My notes of the day I spent on the engine record that it had a reputation for being a very fast running engine and I remember it as riding well. My trip was from Doncaster to Nottingham and back, with a mid-day trip to

Tadcliffe and back to Nottingham. On the way back to Doncaster in the afternoon, I was leaning over the left-hand side, between engine and tender, when my cap blew off. I turned round to face the driver to bemoan the loss of my cap, when he pointed to my feet where lay my cap. He had seen it leave my head, fly up to the rear of the tender, drop into the coal space and sail down through the coal gate on to the engine footplate. On an apprentice's wages in those days, one could not afford to lose a cap!

Next day, as if to set a seal on my affection for steam engines, I rode on no fewer than eight different ones in the course of 10½ hours on duty. On this carefully planned outing I went to Wakefield on a K3, Bradford on an N2, Halifax on an N1, thence on the Pullman back to Bradford on an N2, to Wakefield on a J1, to Pudsey on a C4 (ex-GCR 4-4-2, a 'Jersey Lily'), Leeds on an N1 and finally back to Doncaster on an ex-GCR B5 4-6-0.

It was King's Cross and back the next day on 2553, hauling the two heaviest expresses we worked, namely the 11.04 am to London and the 4.00 pm back – some good hand firing! There was something a little stylish about the London turns, for as we ran into King's Cross there was always a set of men waiting to relieve the Doncaster set who were then able to retire to the loco messroom to consume their 'snap' while the relieving crew took the engine to the loco sidings to turn it and clean the fire, and put on a tub or two of coal in time for the Doncaster men to rejoin their engine preparatory to working the down-road train.

These were good mileage turns, as the return trip amounted to 312 miles and the mileage for a day's pay was only 140, and an hour's pay was added for each additional 15 miles, so a London turn produced well over two days' pay. The link working at Doncaster was arranged in such a way that London turns occupied three days in each week and shorter trips for the other three days, thus spreading out the benefit of mileage earnings. Apprentices, needless to say, did *not* receive mileage payment.

Doncaster shed had a substantial allocation of K3 class 2-6-0s. They were known as 'Jazzers' – a name not unconnected with their mode of progress along the track. They were mainly employed on working fully brake-fitted freight trains; meat and fish were the two loads they principally conveyed, separately of course. Strange though it may seem, knowing the pattern of locomotive utilisation that was commonly adopted after the war, a K3 class engine that took over a fast freight train at Doncaster worked only 80 miles as far as Peterborough, where it came off, to be replaced by a fresh engine and crew. These trains ran at night, so a week of night duty afforded an opportunity to work on them.

K3 No. 2425 approaching Potters Bar with an up express, probably from Cambridge, on 29th April 1939. This engine was built in Scotland by the North British Loco Co. in 1935.

H. C. DOYLE

There was a thrill about riding on the footplate of an engine working a fast train in the dark. No view of the surrounding countryside or the easily-seen signal arm against the sky, but intense concentration on the part of the driver, and often the fireman as well, to pick out the faint glimmer of a green, yellow or red signal light, lit by a flickering oil lamp. In those days few signals had electric lights.

Generally the K3s steamed fairly freely but No 1137 had the reputation of being a bit shy. Sure enough on 23rd June 1932 I booked on at 9.30 pm to ride on the engine to work No 906 up, said to be the hardest up fast freight of them all and the engine booked for the job was 1137. By now, having been firing for some seven weeks, I thought I could make 1137 steam if anyone could, so I took the shovel from Doncaster. The tender was full of a wet mass of fine coal dust, the biggest lump being about one inch in diameter. However, we got on quite nicely for about 45 miles and were past Claypole and beginning the ascent to Peascliffe tunnel and the pressure began to fall. Loath to admit defeat, I kept at it until we got to Grantham and the pressure was down to 150 lb and falling, and reluctantly I handed the shovel to the fireman. We got over Stoke Summit safely and Driver Davey did his best down the bank to Peterborough to make up a few minutes. Having arrived in New England Yard, he went back to do battle (if necessary) with the guard and returned presently to say that said guard had intended to book two minutes to the loco

but had thought better of it. A good, kind man was Driver Davey! But the reader will see what we all thought about time-keeping, even on a freight train; losing time was just not done.

The next night was a very different story. Coming back from Peterborough we had a very heavy train but an excellent engine, No 2765, a K3 only two years old and very recently out of shops after a general overhaul. My notes of that run show that we passed Grantham in 42 minutes after leaving New England and reached Doncaster in 1 hour 45 minutes. Thus the average up Stoke Bank was 38½ mph and for the whole trip nearly 46 mph.

But the most remarkable recollection about this trip was that going up Stoke bank the sides of the shallow cutting were studded with the points of light of many thousands, if not a million or more, glow-worms. Years afterwards, I read that this is quite a rare occurrence, connected with the amorous manifestations of male glow-worms in certain atmospheric conditions. Be that as it may, it was a wonderful sight from the cab of No 2765, much appreciated by the crew of three and the engine itself, for my note also records that the boiler pressure never fell below 180 lb all the way up the bank!

During the next week the 11.04 am to London and the 4.00 pm down were worked by No 2751 *Humorist*, an A3 with left-hand drive and which, in April of that same year, had had a surgical operation carried out on its blastpipe, chimney and smokebox wrapper, which was intended

The cutaway smokebox top of No. 2751 Humorist *represented an effort to lift the exhaust and give drivers of the earlier Pacifics better visibility. The experiment was unsuccessful, and the problem was not solved until the introduction of trough type smoke deflectors in the early 1960s, at the instigation of Peter Townend when he was shedmaster at King's Cross.*
EDITOR'S COLLECTION

Humorist was based at Doncaster shed during the 1930s, and was a regular performer on Great Northern section expresses. It is seen here at Sandy, heading an up Leeds express.

G. H. SOOLE

The surgery at Humorist's *front end did nothing for its appearance; it would be interesting to know what Gresley thought of it.*

to cause an up-draught of air behind the chimney to cause the smoke and exhaust steam to rise clear of the boiler and so give the driver an unimpeded view ahead. This and three further attempts with the same object carried out on the same engine were all unsuccessful. But on the day I rode on 2751 the driver was a tall man of stern demeanour and few words who had become well aware that the reversing screw on the engine was very stiff indeed to turn. The down main line platform at Peterborough was never easy to start from, due to sharp curvature in the track at that point and on this occasion *Humorist* did not live up to its name. In other words, it refused to start. The driver was not amused at having to use all his strength to get into full back gear and, after moving backward a few feet to wind the gear back to full forward, the same thing happened again and this time the driver, not surprisingly, expressed his displeasure in forceful terms. As the moment approached for the third attempt to move forward, the fireman and I stood in silence, hoping for the best but fearing the worst. And the worst it was, for nearly exhausted though he was, the poor driver had to perform the dreadful task all over again. This time we were not sure whether it was what he said to the engine or the fact

that he moved the whole train about a coach length towards London, but with a roar from the chimney as the coupled wheels revolved at speed, moving the train enough to make slight forward progress, we began the journey towards Doncaster. The Duke and Duchess of York (later King George VI and the lady who is now the Queen Mother) were in the train. Whether they were aware of anything unusual I doubt, but I am quite satisfied that they would not have understood what the driver said to his engine.

The first week in July was my last on the footplate, and on the Tuesday morning the District Locomotive Superintendent, Mr George Oakes, sent for me to ask how I was getting on. I told him how much I had enjoyed the last two months and had learned a lot, but I was disappointed that having that very morning asked Inspector Slaughter if I might ride on the engine working the 8.40 am to London (the 7.50 am breakfast train from Leeds), I was not allowed to do so because, said the Inspector, the driver and fireman had all their work cut out to work the train to the new schedule in which the run from passing Grantham to arriving King's Cross was timed at 100 minutes for the 105.5 miles. Mr Oakes did not agree with his Inspector's views and countermanded his order

instantly. Thus it was that for my last three days I rode on the fastest train the depot worked and on the last day the engine was No 2544 *Lemberg* and the driver was Charlie Molson, with his regular engine which he assured me was 'the fastest engine ever built'. My notebook relates that we ran from Grantham pass to Peterborough pass in $26\frac{1}{2}$ minutes (average 65.7 mph) and from Peterborough to Huntingdon in 16 minutes (65 mph) which, said Charlie, nobody would ever better. It was not bad, considering the severe speed restriction through Peterborough, but neither times nor speeds must be compared with present day High Speed Trains, which have 4,500 horsepower to play with compared with an A3 which would have been hard put to it to produce about 1,750 indicated horsepower and much less at the drawbar. No 2544 was one of the first two A1 class Pacifics rebuilt under H. N. Gresley with 220 lb per sq in boilers and, in this case, 19 in diameter cylinders.

So, on 8th July 1932 my Salad Days in Steam ended and I returned to work in the Doncaster Plant Works. I had done something over 7,800 miles on the footplate and enjoyed every one of them! I learned a lot, too.

O2 class No. 3501, with a down goods train, approaching Greenwood box and the two-track bottleneck through to Potters Bar, in May 1926.   GRESLEY SOCIETY COLLECTION

RECOLLECTIONS OF SOME LESSER GRESLEY LOCOMOTIVES

GERARD FIENNES

Eight O2s were built at Doncaster in 1932 for coal traffic between the new Whitemoor yard and Temple Mills. One was No. 2959, seen here at March, coupled to a 4,200 gallon tender from a J38 0—6—0, after it had been realised that these locos did not need the water scoop equipment with which the larger tenders were fitted.

GRESLEY SOCIETY COLLECTION

SOME of our readers may recall that my talk to the society a few years ago on how the user looked (with a worm's eye view and with total respect) at Gresley was received with entire politeness but with something less than enthusiasm. Let me assure you that here I shall not stray into flights of fancy as to what would have been the outcome if Gresley had been an electrifier or a dieseliser. These recollections have to do very largely with Gresley's impact on the former Great Eastern in the late 1920s and 1930s, particularly on the movement of freight.

Sir Michael Barrington-Ward, Superintendent of the Western Section, user of the Pacifics and K3s, used to look over the fence at the Eastern Section and talk about 'that tramway'. Through Whitemoor, after the new mechanised yards were built in 1929–31, there passed over 3,000 wagons a day in each direction. The 'Great Northern' could not match that. So it gave me undiluted, and somewhat malign, pleasure that some years later our Grand Old Man Mauldin was appointed to the General Managership of the LNER's Southern Area and to be in his office when B-W came in to offer his congratulations. 'So you're the lucky lad, are you?' he said, and swept out.

For the moment, back to 1931 when I went to Whitemoor as Assistant Yardmaster. For the 3,000 wagons a day in the up direction we had a range of former

Great Eastern engines ranging from the J15, some still wet steamers, in Class 3, to the J20 in Class 6. When the new up yard was opened, we received sixteen 3-cylinder O2s and were year by year being re-equipped with class 5 J39s. The O2s were confined to the run between Whitemoor and Temple Mills.

The range of load lay between 33 of mineral for a J15 and 65 of mineral for an O2. Since the load was calculated on the basis of 10-ton wagons, the usual train for an O2 was 59–65 of mineral, and if we could get, say, sixteen trains a day hauled by O2s, we shifted about 1,000 wagons with these sixteen engines. It was horses' work. As you know, you 'rude mechanicals', an engine may look well on the drawing board; a picture coming out of the works; a tough workhorse backing on to her train; but unless she will steam she is as sounding brass and a clashing cymbal. Indeed, she will not back on to too many trains because the driver, on one pretext or another, will not take her off shed. So it was with the O2s.

I remember in 1934 when the Chief Controller at Cambridge, H. F. Sanderson, District Superintendent, had me under the harrow for our Net Ton Miles per Engine Hour (an important measure of performance in those days) being not up to his requirements. So the Chief Freight Train Clerk and I settled down with a bunch of Guards' Journals. 'Look', said Frank Stone in his gravelly voice, 'another ruddy J15.'

And we found that on that day only seven of our sixteen O2s had worked up from Whitemoor to Temple Mills. So we put in a special system of control. Each engine was 'targeted' to do a round trip and a half in a day between Whitemoor and Temple Mills – 250 miles. Ambitious you may say, but it was not more than twelve hours on the road, which left twelve hours for two turn-rounds, and maintenance. We did not achieve it, of course, but we went a long way towards it. And we and our Net Ton Miles escaped the wrath of God. Funnily enough, we never heard anything about bad steaming on a Saturday if March Town were playing at home and Masher May was on the front of a truck train five minutes in front of an express. I have been in an old Great Eastern brake van, not by reputation one of the more comfortable rides, clocking 63 mph through Great Chesterford and Whittlesford – where we should have stopped for examination – but not on a Saturday, not behind Masher May, and not when March Town were playing at home.

In those days we had a lot of wagons with grease axleboxes. Trains stopped for examination every 40 miles or so. Behind the examiner walked a lad with a can of fat and a sort of spatula with which he fired extra grease into the axlebox. I always thought the danger was fairly imaginary. A hot axle box was an easy defect to detect and remedy. First it got very warm and emitted a thin stream of grey-blue smoke.

The J39 0–6–0 was numerically Gresley's largest class, totalling 289 in all, built between 1926 and 1941. It was designed at Darlington, where by far the largest number were built, including No. 2973, in 1932, here seen coupled to the smaller group standard 3,500 gallon tender.
GRESLEY SOCIETY COLLECTION

J39 No. 64955 approaching Grantham from the south with a goods train, sometime in the 1950s.

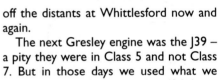

The J39s were generally a popular class with the operating staff, powerful for their size and with a fair turn of speed. This picture shows No. 64876 in charge of a horsebox special near Grantham.
JOHN F. CLAY

This wafted along the train and came to the nose of the guard who looked out and, according to the distance of the next booked stop, decided whether to stop the train and detach the wagon or whether to go on. If he decided to stop, he applied Rule 127 by which he screwed on his hand brake, released it suddenly, screwed it on again, released it ... thereby plucking through the couplings at the driver's tail. The fireman looked back, the guard held out a red light or flag. The driver stopped. They conferred and decided what to do. Or he used some less legitimate method such as taking off his tail lamp when passing a signal box.

Alternatively, a signalman might have detected the hot box and sent 'stop and examine train' forward, with a like result. If, however, neither detected it then the next stage was that it burst into flames. There was still no danger because the journal was still turning in grease. The danger came when the flames went out and the axle was turning dry in the box. Then the journal end burnt off and down went one end of the wagon. I remember one derailment only from this cause, between Bury St Edmunds and Thurston. About 40 wagons and brake van went down a twenty-foot embankment. Spectacular! But there was little risk in pulling

off the distants at Whittlesford now and again.

The next Gresley engine was the J39 – a pity they were in Class 5 and not Class 7. But in those days we used what we were given and did not say dreadful things to Chief Mechanical Engineers like 'I want an engine which will haul x tons at y miles an hour between Whitemoor and Temple Mills'. With that reservation the J39 was a splendid workhorse. My favourite railway sound is the half-strangled half-obscene sneeze of the J39's snifting valve as she got under way. But there was nothing half-strangled about the way they would haul a coal train or fly with an express goods. And they would steam all day.

In the 1930s we still had the agriculture of East Anglia by rail. East of Whitemoor a fleet of J39s took care of it. Now and again I, taking my Chief Controllership seriously, would spend an evening in the box at Whittlesford or Chesterford or Audley End. From 11 pm onwards until 3 am, they poured up the Cambridge line. The Whittlesea meat, the 11.10, 11.20, 11.30, 11.40 and 12.05 Coldham's Lane, the 9.05 Whitemoor, the Lynn, and finally the cabbages 11.10 and 11.30 from Spalding on their way to Spitalfields and Stratford markets. The J39s in full career pounding up Chesterford bank with the long line of vans shouldering and shaking behind

K3 2–6–0s were turned out at both Darlington and Doncaster, together with a large number built by contractors. No. 2443 was one of an order for twenty placed with the North British Loco Co. in 1935, and is seen here going well in charge of a fast goods train, near Corby Glen, on 25th July 1939.

H. C. DOYLE

them exuded a great sense of urgency and exhilaration. I remember that in one month the punctuality of our express freight was better than that of our express passenger. It is, maybe, a curious aspect of drivers that they will fly with an engine which is rough – and the J39s were really rough at speed – provided she will steam.

Nevertheless, they had a fault which led many years later to them being taken off passenger trains. They were not only rough but they rolled. So of course did the GN Atlantics but I know little about them. After the war there was more than one instance of a J39 taking a passenger train down an embankment. As Chairman of the Joint Enquiries, I loyally pinned the blame on the Civil Engineer for not refetling the track after relaying or some such. But in my soul I felt sure that if those trains had been hauled by 1500s they would not have finished up at the bottom of a bank with their paws in the air.

It was in 1937, when I went to Liverpool Street as Chief Freight Trains Clerk to Colonel Mauldin, that the weakness of the J39 became apparent, namely that she was not in Class 7. The revelation of how much could be saved by the greater use of engines as expressed in the targeting of

the O2s and more recently by the Bonus workings on Teesside had made me very conscious of low mileages. To work 66 miles from Norwich to Whitemoor, then to stable the engine and go into lodge for nine hours before working 66 miles back was the first outstanding nonsense. Therefore we should work out-and-home from Norwich to Whitemoor and back, potentially saving at least six sets of men and four engines. But to do so required upgrading of the coal trains from Whitemoor from Class C, say 20 mph, to Class A, 30 mph. Luckily, grease axleboxes were now a thing of the past. The load of the J39 at Class A was pitiful. So I cast my covetous eyes over the fence at the Western Section's K3s with which we could lift 45 of mineral at Class A. Now at that time the head of the freight section on the Western side was Sergei Molotov whose response to any request or approach was as you remember 'Nyet'. So it was with little hope and great humility that I asked for the transfer of six K3s to Norwich. Inexplicably, the man turned into Freddie Fielder and within a month we had them. We located them at Norwich, thinking that Norwich, who now had an engine of matchless power, would run those trains

like cockbirds; and so it proved – express goods out, coal trains home. And however rough the K3s were, and even in Gresley's book I have never ridden on a rougher, they wore it with equanimity and almost enthusiasm. Curiously enough, although the K3s were far rougher than the J39s, they did not derail so easily. On one occasion the 6.50 pm March Parcels came off the road at Cowbit, and once, after the war, at Tottenham, a driver was suddenly aware that a tyre was bowling along like a hoop beside him, but he brought the train gently to a standstill and still on the road.

Finally, we had some K2s. No 1754 is graven on my heart. In maybe 1949, when we were running, on a Saturday, about 20 trains an hour out of Liverpool Street to Southend, Clacton, Walton and Yarmouth, 1754 lay down on the main line on two Saturdays running, short of Romford, and gave up the ghost. I asked E. H. (Teddy) Ker at Stratford Loco never to turn her out for passenger work again, but he did the next Saturday. But she never got near a passenger train.

I have rambled on too long and am straying into passenger work, which is another story.

LNER EXPERIENCES
THE DRIVER'S STORY

CHARLIE PEACHEY
(as told to the late J. M. Craig)

I was born in Cambridgeshire, between Wisbech and March, and worked on a 600-acre farm before becoming an engine cleaner at King's Cross when I was not quite 17. You were supposed to be 18, but in those days you did not have to show your birth certificate. I was an engine cleaner for 2 years and 8 months, then passed as a fireman. After 12 years and 9 months as a fireman I passed as a driver. I had been a driver for 33 years when I retired in 1942, at the age of 64. I enjoyed the whole of my 47 years on the railway, and I am enjoying my retirement. Good workers live a long time.

As an engine cleaner I earned 2s. 6d. a day. It made no difference whether you were on the day or night shift in those days – there was no extra pay for night work. When you rose you took on to clean an engine by yourself. The top pay for engine cleaning was 3s. 4d. a day and that was for cleaning an 8-footer; we had two of these at King's Cross and several with 7 ft 6 in wheels. That was not a hard job – you could do it in six hours and sometimes I would get mine cleaned and be home for breakfast and not have to go back. It had to be done thoroughly or the driver would complain – the drivers used to 'own' the engines.

I liked being a fireman; you do not have to work so hard as on cleaning, but you have to use your brains more, in placing the coal, etc. A fireman must do as the driver says. Firemen sometimes do a little driving when on shunting engines, but must be careful about it. When I was a driver I would let my fireman drive for a bit while I shovelled for him. At 55 I could still do it as well as the young ones could. I considered firing as artistic work, of which you could be proud, and you did a good hard day's work then. The engines were kept beautifully clean. When I was a fireman our largest engines were the Atlantic type, and they were very good engines for the express passenger work, running to Leeds and back the same day. When I was a driver the engines began to get bigger and more powerful and it was

No. 4468 Mallard *climbing past Belle Isle on its way back to its home shed of Doncaster.*

COLLECTION A. B. COLLINS

No. 2563 was still named William Whitelaw *when this picture was taken of it heading the down non-stop 'Flying Scotsman' into Newcastle Central, in 1928 or 1929. The loco was named after the then Chairman of the LNER, the grandfather of the present Lord Whitelaw. In 1941 it was renamed* Tagalie, *when the name was transferred to A4 No. 4462.*   AUTHOR'S COLLECTION

a great pleasure to be a driver on such good engines, and they could do their work easily when handled properly.

When you have had time shunting in goods and coal yards you get other odd jobs – on the South London, climbing up Ludgate Hill, out to Hither Green, Battersea and Herne Hill. In these days we ran local trains from High Barnet into Victoria on the London to Brighton line, and those were good jobs. I had a spell on the local side tanks running into Moorgate and back to High Barnet, Cuffley, Hatfield and Alexandra Palace. It was ten hours a day as fireman, and again when I began as a driver. It is on jobs like those that you get to know the value of the condenser, when coming up through some of the tunnels, especially the single ones like King's Cross Met. to King's Cross suburban. The smoke is enough to choke you if you do not use the condenser.

You do not learn all railway work out of the book, though you have to learn the rules from the rule book which you are given when passed as a fireman. The main thing is being able to handle your engine and knowing the signals, and running the train to time. If you miss a signal in snow or fog you go slow till you find the next signal. You also have fogmen to guide you, but they might not have got to their posts if a fog had come down suddenly. If you 'miss' a distant signal you make sure of seeing the home signal.

When you knew the road, even fog did not make much difference because you knew the sounds. Should you lose yourself you would soon know by the feeling of the route. I used to know almost all the trees between King's Cross and Edinburgh, and what was in this or that field last year.

You feel tired about two in the morning (when everyone should be asleep) and you would stand up to keep awake. One night my first job after being off three weeks with 'flu was the express goods from Grantham. I could feel myself getting dozy, and my eyes would keep shutting. Going through Biggleswade the express from London was coming. There was a bit of a curve, and I saw one headlight which seemed to be going red. It woke me up.

As a driver you must go back over all the same ground as when you were a fireman.

I went on the main line work before my proper time, as after working the tank links, I was 'pinched' for main line work. Some drivers used to be content to work in goods and coal yards and would not go any further, because of the lodging out once you were on the main line jobs.

A driver starts by shunting in the yards, and in the shed, taking engines away from the coal stages, and then does local work: passenger and goods trains to South London, Hitchin, Peterborough and Grantham. But to get a regular job you have to take your turn in seniority. If one driver refuses one of these jobs the next in turn gets it. When I started on the 'Flying Scotsman' 19 drivers senior to me refused the

job. That was on the summer working, from July 1st to the second week in September, and I was a year after Arthur Taylor and worked opposite to George Haygreen. The train was then non-stop from King's Cross at 10 o'clock to Edinburgh, arriving at 5.30 pm (393 miles), and the same coming back, and it was a very nice trip. The King's Cross driver and fireman used to work the train from King's Cross to ten miles beyond York, and then the Edinburgh men would come forward and take charge. Next morning we reported at Haymarket shed at 8.30 am to help the Edinburgh men to prepare the engine and to see that everything had been done properly – that the coal on the tender was all safe and would not roll off, and that the tank was full of water, and that the water scoop was alright, as we picked up water six times between Edinburgh and King's Cross. There was one trough between Edinburgh and Newcastle, and five troughs from there to London.

On the down run my fireman and I would go back to the front third class compartment which was for the crew only. After washing and dressing we went to the dining car for dinner, which was free. Soon after crossing the Border Bridge we went into tea, though we were not supposed to have it, and tea was also taken to the men on the engine. We were ready when we got off the train at Edinburgh for an evening out, having earned two and a half days' pay.

In the winter months King's Cross men used to work the 'Flying Scotsman' to Newcastle and then come off with the engine and go to Gateshead Loco and lodge and work the 8.15 am up next day, stopping at Durham, Darlington, York and Grantham, being into London at 1.20 pm. The following week we worked a 'Parly' train to Peterborough and an express train back, and had no lodging away. This was a good arrangement, being away for a week and then at home for a week. When the non-stop finished at the end of that summer I had to go back on the night express goods trains for a month. Then one of the top link drivers was taken ill and finished work, so I took his place in the top link and had ten years in it; it was beautiful work with the 'Flying Scotsman', 'Silver Jubilee', and other Scottish trains. I had *Fairway* for two years in the Newcastle Link and my home in North Finchley is called 'Fairway'. There is a lot in using an engine properly, and *Fairway* was a beauty.

I was never in the Pullman Link, because of going straight from express goods trains into the Top Link.

One day I was on the 'Flying Scotsman' from Edinburgh to King's Cross when Will Fyffe was on the train. One of the dining car attendants was booking his time for lunch, when Will Fyffe asked him if he could go on to the engine for a few minutes. The attendant said he would go and ask the King's Cross driver, in the crews' compartment. I told him I would go and ask the Scots driver who said 'yes' when he heard who it was. I fetched Will Fyffe out of the train and he came on to the engine for about ten minutes, just as we were crossing the Border Bridge. Will Fyffe said he had better be getting back to his lunch, but I asked him if he would like to stay and see us pick up water. Then I took him back to the dining car. He said 'Perhaps you don't know who I am?', so I said 'No', although of course I did know. He said 'You may have heard me sing "The Song of the Railway Guard", now I can sing a "Song of the Railway Driver".' And he shook hands with a pound note there, and said 'Here's ten bob for the boys on the engine, and ten bob for you and your mate'.

Another day at Edinburgh a lady was seeing her friends off to King's Cross. She was sitting in the train with them when the train started – there's no noise or fuss when the non-stop leaves – and she could not get off before it left the platform. She had to go on to King's Cross. Either the ticket collector or the guard made out a note, tied it to a lump of coal, and threw it to a signalman, blowing a whistle to attract attention. Just before York a message was brought to me before I went on to the engine and I was told to get to London four or five minutes early if possible, so that the lady could catch a train back to Edinburgh leaving at 5.30 as we were due in. I kept time as far as Peterborough; and then aimed to be a minute early through Huntingdon, two minutes early through Hitchin, three or four minutes early through Hatfield – you could do it easy as pie – and the lady caught the 5.30. She had a nice trip, Edinburgh to Edinburgh via King's Cross, 786 miles.

There was only one occasion when we had to stop the non-stop. We were in the crews' compartment actually, the Scotsmen being in charge near the end of the run. We got to within 20 miles of Edinburgh when the middle big end got hot and the train had to be stopped. We changed engines and got a goods engine, but that ran short of steam and there was another stop to take a pilot.

One day we nearly had to stop after Doncaster, when the signal was set for us to go on the Lincoln branch. But I whistled hard and put on the brakes and the signalman put us right just in time on to the main line, and we did not stop. A 'Parly' train normally left Doncaster ahead of us, but was still in the station as we passed, so the signalman's mistake was understandable.

I had some champion firemen, and if they were not good when they came they were when they left. To fire from King's Cross to Newcastle, 268 miles, with a 500 ton train, is a good day's work, but you would hear few grumbles as most firemen liked the work, and the pay was good, with mileage money. I used to do a bit on the uphill stretch from Essendine to Grantham, and let the fireman have something to eat.

On one Sunday we were to travel passenger to Edinburgh for the first non-stop run up and were walking towards King's Cross when the fireman said 'There's no hurry – the train doesn't leave until 11.30.'

Quicksilver in repose at Peterborough on 18th October 1936 during the series of brake trials which took place on Sundays at this time.

H. M. HOATHER

A few minutes later we saw it go out; the fireman had been calculating by the summer working which did not in fact start until the Monday. We caught a train half an hour later which took us to Newcastle. Then we caught a special on its way back from Whitley Bay to Newcastle and Edinburgh, otherwise we would not have got in until about three o'clock next morning.

At first there were only six drivers in the top link, for three Newcastle and three Peterborough workings. When the 'Jubilee' started, two more sets were added, and with the 'Coronation' another set. And then we got the 'Coronation' only one week in six. There was no strain in driving a streamliner, all you had to do was to take it easy and not worry.

Going down, the 'Coronation' stopped at York and arrived at Newcastle 7.58, two minutes short of four hours. Then the Scotsmen got on and we were free until 6.30 the next night when we relieved the Edinburgh men on the up train, due in King's Cross at 10.30. Coming back we would have about five hours on duty, signing on at Gateshead at 6 pm and walking to Newcastle station, and for that we would be paid for $16\frac{1}{2}$ hours, and lodge money. We would be relieved on arrival at King's Cross station and booked on next day at 2.45 at King's Cross shed. If we were to start from Newcastle on Monday we took down the Sunday 1 pm from King's Cross. For the 'Silver Jubilee' we signed on at 4 pm and left the shed at 5 o'clock. Leaving King's Cross at 5.30 we would reach Newcastle at 9.30. We would uncouple, take the engine to Gateshead Loco shed, examine her to see that everything was alright (no hot bearings), then enter in the book any repairs required to make her right. I used to like to run in two minutes before time and was noted for arriving at 1.59 with the 'Jubilee'; two minutes early was good timekeeping, but to be three minutes early was not. The 'Jubilee' was not quite so heavy as the 'Coronation', and was easy to run, and I was never late with it. Fancy anyone refusing a job like that – I would like to drive it again!

Very often after you had been on the 'Jubilee' for a week you would be sent to York on the Saturday with the 'Scarborough Flier' and back with the return train. That was two days' pay for 11 hours' work.

On a down trip on the 'Jubilee' between Grantham and Newark I looked behind

Since working the first 'Coronation' from King's Cross to Edinburgh, on 5th July 1937, Commonwealth of Australia remained on this duty, down one day and up the next, with hardly an interruption until 24th September. Here it is seen leaving York on the down train on 26th July 1937.
H. C. DOYLE

and noticed a tender axle box smoking. Pulling up at the first signal box, I asked if the 'Parly' train was still at Newark. 'Tell him to be ready, we want him', I said. We changed engines there and picked up an Atlantic, but we had to change engines again at Doncaster as the Atlantic was loose between the tender and the engine, and coal kept jumping down and really would have been dangerous at speed. We got a Pacific for the rest of the run to Newcastle, and lost 25 minutes on the trip, having made up some time after York.

I only once smelt the pear drop and violet smell of the 'stink bomb', showing that the middle big end was hot. (The bomb exploded if a certain temperature were reached, and gave off a strong odour.) The fireman got more of the smell on his side and said it was only the smell of the sweet factories we were passing after Doncaster; I got only a whiff at first. At Selby the smell was unmistakable, and we went slowly on to York and got a fresh engine. Apparently the smell still had not disappeared after two days! When the fitter took the big end down he said the journal was only slightly damaged. There was good stuff in them.

On one trip with the 'Jubilee' from King's Cross to Newcastle on 17th June 1936, Mr T. Adkins, a writer in *The Railway Magazine*, came down and spoke to me on No 2511 *Silver King*, and asked if I would get to Darlington (first stop) a few minutes early, as he wanted to catch a train back to York, due out as we were due in. We left King's Cross two minutes late, owing

to signals, and there were speed restrictions at New Barnet owing to a newly rebuilt underbridge. We were four or five minutes late by then. There was no speedometer on the engine that night, so I thought I can go a bit hard now – nobody will know anything. It was better to be behind time rather than ahead, to get a clear road. We were not supposed to exceed 90, with 80 maximum through Hitchin. About three miles after passing Hitchin we were going hard, but it was not until afterwards that I heard we had done 104 mph, or about 14 mph too fast according to instructions: we were four minutes early into Darlington. Mr Adkins took full details of the run down and sent me a copy of his record, asking if he could put it in *The Railway Magazine*. I thought that when it came out I would get the sack. It was a lovely piece of road – no bumping. The dining car crew were pleased with the run, and they would have been the first to complain of any unsteadiness. Everyone was pleased, and a traffic inspector said 'It's alright, you've advertised the train'. The letter from Mr Adkins said 'One of the finest trips ever run on an English railway'.

The 'Jubilee' was allowed two sections in which to stop. If you did not stop in the first you would not be punished, and could use the second, although you could stop always in the one section, as the train was light.

Once at a dinner for enginemen from sheds all over the LNER system, Inspector Holder cracked us up. 'No other railway

Dominion of Canada about to start away from Grantham with the summer relief to the 'Flying Scotsman', known unofficially as the 'Junior Scotsman'. 29th July 1938.
JOHN F. CLAY

can touch the Great Northern', he said. 'In fact, one driver here can run a train to a second.' Then I went to the bar with a friend, and another driver was there talking to an inspector. He said 'Holder seems to like Peachey. If I couldn't drive a train like him I'd eat my hat.' The inspector said, 'You can't touch him!'

I had No 2001 *Cock o' the North* first on my normal turns of duty that week, which were a 'Parly' train to Peterborough and back on an express on three days, and on the 1.20 as far as Grantham and back with another express on three days. On Monday of the next week we had her on a trial run to Lincoln drawing a 665-ton train with dynamometer car. All the important people were in the car next to the engine. I had to work the engine as they said. We stopped at Peterborough for Mr Gresley to come on. The first instructions were 'Regulator wide open, full gear, leave it there for one minute ($\frac{1}{2}$ mile), now pull up 10%'. I said to Mr Gresley 'We're not going a long way like this'. He said: 'Please yourself – they won't know behind anyway'. After the water troughs we got to Essendine, still climbing a little. When the engine came round and

was steaming well I said 'They can have what they want now'. Mr Gresley was a gentleman who never interfered with your work when he was riding on the engine with you. He told me he was on an engine in Germany a fortnight ago and said the engine was doing 100 mph, so I said 'You had not got 650 tons to pull, I know'. Mr Gresley said: 'Open out and see what she will do.' He was very pleased, as we were doing 65–70 mph when climbing the bank which is called the 'Old 100' about five miles from Grantham. We went about four miles beyond Grantham on the Lincoln road and turned on a triangle and set back on the other end of the train ready for London. The inspectors had not thought of getting any coal forward, and no arrangement had been made for anybody to come out from Grantham. One of the inspectors, in his bowler hat, tried to get coal down, but could not. So on the way back the fireman had to get it in the tender, while one of the inspectors (who had been a driver) took over firing, but he did not do well and we were losing steam. So, although it meant breaking rule 14, I let the inspector sit on the driving seat to handle the engine while I got coal down

and my fireman looked after the fire. Then I said to the inspector 'I'll take charge, the way you're paying the engine we'll have to stop at Hatfield for coal.' We had practically no coal left at King's Cross, and wasn't I dirty? I was given 10/- at the end of the run, and passed it to the fireman. One of the inspectors invited me to stay on the engine for a week – but I had had enough, and was losing a day's pay compared with going to Newcastle. So he gave instructions for my engine to be ready for the next day. *Cock o' the North* went to France for trials, but I did not choose to go with her; they needed two firemen on some of the trials! *Cock o' the North* would have pulled anything, even if they had hung on King's Cross.

Prince Olaf once joined the train at Newcastle. The station master brought him down and asked if he would like to get on the engine, and he said yes that was just what he wanted to do. He asked me 'What horsepower is the engine, driver?' Well I did not know, I had never thought about it, so I changed the subject and told him the boiler pressure. When we arrived at King's Cross Prince Olaf saluted me as he passed the engine, just as King

George V always used to when he had to pass the engine if the train had come into platform 2. (If it came into platform 1 the red carpet was so placed that he left the station without passing the engine.)

There was a gentleman timing a down run one day when we had to give up a Pacific at Grantham with a 540 ton train. We got Atlantic No 3285, and in the course of the run to York had $3\frac{1}{2}$ min permanent way checks, but we were into York in just under 90 min. The Atlantics were grand engines, but I did not have them much.

I was driving the 'Aberdonian', leaving King's Cross at 7.30, during the worst week of air raids. We had to drive at 15 mph all the way to Grantham — seven hours for the 105 miles and we would arrive two to three hours late (what a change from the two hours schedule). When we left King's Cross the loud-speakers were calling for people to join the train or else go in the dugout. I would

tend to speed up a bit if nothing seemed to be happening, but a signalman would stop the train if it went too hard.

There were no lights in stations, on locomotives or on turntables. It was quite dark in Grantham station, and in the loco yard it seemed that my fireman and I were the only two people in Grantham. When we went to turn the engine we could not see one another. After we had finished getting the engine ready the shed foreman would come round and tell us what train we were to work back to King's Cross. We had to coal our own engine because everybody else would be in the dugout.

We arrived back at King's Cross one Sunday morning (we were due in at 5.30 and arrived at 10.30) to find that a bomb had dropped on the booking office on No 10 platform and had killed 13 people, mostly soldiers on duty there. It *was* a dirty unhappy-looking place, the whole of the station being covered with bits and pieces.

I have a feeling at times that I would like to have a ride on an engine of an express train again, but still they are not so clean as they used to be, when with a good fireman it was a sheer joy to drive them.

Eric Neve comments: 'When Charlie Peachey was on the Peterborough turn, 4.15 pm down and 9.25 back at King's Cross, he would nip into the buffet at King's Cross for a quick pint before catching the 9.45 local home. Some of us youngsters would join him in this train for a yarn. One impetuous youth once said "So and so did 100 down Stoke last week". Quick as a flash came the reply "What of it? We always do 100 down Stoke", with which the fireman agreed.

'I remember one morning when Charlie took the Grand National Pullman to Aintree, passing New Southgate as I waited for the 8.06 up to King's Cross. I would have liked to have heard about that trip!'

Eric also advises that the tender box incident on the down 'Jubilee' was 17th August 1937, and that the Pacifics involved were 2510 and 2596.

Regarding the 17th June, 1936 trip, Mr Peachey called the shuttling passenger Mr J. Atkins, but as C.J.A. referred to him as Mr T. Adkins we have so called him. I cannot say which is correct. – (Ed.)

A PERSONAL ACCOUNT OF 'THE SILVER JUBILEE' TRIAL RUN
DRIVER ARTHUR TAYLOR

IN my opinion, *Silver Link* was a grand engine, and easily the best of the streamliners, as she was hand-made, and not mass produced. She became my engine; I thought the world of her, and enjoyed travelling at really high speed. I nearly missed the trial run, but Mr Groom, the Locomotive Running Superintendent, wanted the driver to be someone who had experience of the engine and knew the road well, so I took the train.

There were altogether four people on the footplate, and about Southgate Mr Groom said 'You aren't doing so well.' I said that a full head of steam was necessary and the gauge was registering only 220 lb, whereas it should have been 250 lb, so Mr Groom told Fireman Luty to get down to it and get the pressure up. The practice to be adopted was to fire and then let the coal burn through, and not make the mistake of putting too much on the fire when we really got going. The only 'bind'

we felt was at Hitchin, and I remarked to Mr Groom that it was too fast to go through that place, but all right elsewhere; apparently we were doing almost 100 mph there, and were later to cover 25 miles at 107.5 mph and maintain an average of 100 mph for 43 miles, with a highest speed of 112.5 mph, which was reached on two occasions. The running, except when we were going through Hitchin, was ever so smooth. Mr Gresley came through the corridor tender and told me what speed we'd achieved. Quite frankly I didn't think we'd been going much above 90 mph and apparently it was smoother on the engine than in the train. Mr Gresley asked me if *Royal Lancer* could have done what *Silver Link* did. I said 'Yes, but I shouldn't have cared for the ride, being afraid of the reversing lever leaving its foundations.' She had twice been in Plant without that matter (which was beyond the King's Cross fitters) being rectified. The floor

wasn't strong enough to hold the standard, while the bolts were tight but not tight enough. So Mr Gresley got out his note-book to put down a reminder, and sure enough the job was done properly next time 4476 was in Plant. When Mr Gresley asked what I thought of *Silver Link*, I said she was splendid, and that I was glad of the stronger springs, and no more bashing the sides of the frames going round Offord, where I'd wondered whether the frame would break. 90 mph down the banks was about the limit with the earlier Pacifics. I consider 100 mph quite practicable provided there are no speed restrictions and that the track is sufficiently strong to stand the additional wear and tear. I did enjoy that run, and word must have been sent from Grantham of what had been done, as it was like a gala day when we came into King's Cross, and judging by the crowds, it seemed as if royalty were expected!

MEMORIES OF COLWICK

SID CHECKLEY

THE following notes are some random thoughts about some of the locomotives I worked on as a fitter at Colwick in the period at the end of and following the 1939–45 War. The engines were almost without exception in a deplorable condition, having been 'run into the ground' during the war.

The H2 tank engines in their Colwick days were, to say the least, on their last legs, (or wheels). They were very unpopular with the footplate staff and maintenance staff alike. One of them, 6416, if my memory serves me right, was in the shop every few days for lifting with one or the other coupled boxes hot. It was rumoured that with 6421, one had only to stand on the front framing and whistle and the main steam pipes would come out of the smoke box of their own accord, they were out so often. The reason was that the smoke box saddle was loose on the main frames; consequently, it was almost impossible to keep the main steam pipe joints tight. These engines were very lightly built compared with the GN or GC engines, and the work they were expected to perform in the Nottingham area was somewhat heavy. They were gradually superseded by the N2 tanks. The last one finished its days on a local horse and cart job known as Lawrence's Pilot. This consisted of ambling around the local private sidings. As an aside, quite a number of famous engines finished their lives on this job. I have been told that GNR 264, the last Ivatt single-wheeler, was one of these.

Another notable type at Colwick at this time was the GN 'Atlantic'. These engines were in a very run-down condition at this time, but still took part in the local passenger workings. I had one in the shop at Colwick for valve and piston examination. This was 3282; while she was in the shop her number was changed to 2811. This was in February 1946. We took her bogie out to make more space to get the valves out. For some reason these bogies always carried a peculiar smell. The valves were balanced 'D' type with spring strips to hold the valves on the steam chest faces. The valves were made of a type of phosphor-bronze and to say they were heavy is putting it mildly. Putting them back in the

steam chest entailed holding the valve buckle, the valve and the spring strips. This was achieved with a thin steel plate and a lot of effort.

Getting the coupled wheels out of these engines could be a job as, for some reason or other, all the service pipes ran under the axles, i.e. vacuum, exhaust injector, steam pipe for steam sand ejectors, vacuum pipe for lock-on reversing gear. These all had to be removed before we started to remove the wheels.

At this time there was a working from Sheffield that arrived on the shed front at about mid-day and this was often a GN 'Atlantic'. For some reason this engine always seemed to need the brakes adjusting on the carrier wheels. These wheels had a separate vacuum cylinder, from the coupled wheels. The coupled wheels had two 21 in cylinders under the leading coupled axle. I never knew any of these engines to give boiler trouble.

We had a few GC 'Atlantics', mostly engaged on the Nottingham–Grantham service. One of these distinguished itself by coming apart from its tender in Gonerby Tunnel. Another of the same class (I think it was 2902) was derailed in Nottingham Victoria on Goose Fair Saturday evening. Chaos reigned. This was due to a bogie defect. An interesting sight was to be seen when we removed the coupled wheels from one of the Woodford GC engines; it was standing in the sidings on just the bogie and carrier wheels. The GC 'Atlantics' had 'D' valve steam chests. Occasionally the steam chest joints would blow. To renew these joints one had to lay on one's side between the steam chests over the top of the bogie frame and manoeuvre the steam chest cover off the studs, clean the joint faces, make a new joint and heave the cover back into place. Another feature of note, was that the carrier axle union had four axle boxes, two outside the frame and two inside. The inside ones had coil springs. The hangers on these were known to slack off, with the result that the boxes were just riding, not carrying any weight.

Another type of engine that caused us some pain at this time was the J39. These engines were really powerful for six-

wheelers and they were certainly overworked. During this period we had several of them in the shop for tyre turning. This was a convenient time to do a valve and piston examination, as there was space to work. Re-entering the gudgeon pin on these engines could be entertaining. This was put in from outside the engine through a hole in the frame. It was necessary to line up the holes in the crosshead, two loose slide blocks and the small end. With one man outside holding the gudgeon pin and one man underneath adjusting five components, the running commentary was often worth hearing. Some of the J39s had vacuum brakes on the engine and tender. The vacuum cylinders on the engine were 27 in diameter and made of cast iron. Renewing the rolling ring on these cylinders called for a steady hand and a powerful neck as the easiest way to enter these pistons was by balancing the outfit on one's head like Covent Garden porters. Various screw jigs were tried but we usually came back to the muscle methods.

During the early 1950s these engines were sent to Gorton Works for overhaul. Gorton Works at that time were assembling electric locos for the Manchester–Sheffield electrification and could not cope with all the J39s sent to them. Some of them, therefore, were sent to Derby Works. This was not a popular move at Derby as the piece-work prices were different and the methods of construction were different to anything they had. After shopping at Derby the engines were sent to Colwick for running in and returning to their home depot. This was the cause of our troubles. One thing was the snifting valve. On the J39s this was on the superheater header casting in the smoke box. It was secured to the main casting by six $\frac{5}{8}$ in studs, nutted round the sides. What happened at Derby I can only guess, but nearly every engine came back to us with the nuts missing, and the valve casting just dropped on loose. Consequently, there was a great steam blow inside the smoke box.

Those engines fitted with Westinghouse air pumps were nearly all in trouble after shopping. Various officials

J39 No. 2943 at Nottingham Victoria in the late 1930s with a freshly refurbished King's Cross suburban articulated set in use on an excursion.
T. G. HEPBURN, RAIL ARCHIVE STEPHENSON

came from the works to see these engines after shopping but the troubles gradually died away when the locos were transferred to other works.

An interesting point with the J39s was that it was possible to assemble the valve gear wrongly. If the eccentrics or rods were taken down for any reason, say for removing the driving wheels, care had to be taken when putting them back to follow the marking on the rods, i.e. L.F., R.B. etc. Failure to do so could have interesting results. I've seen this happen. On one occasion the fitter got one side right and one side wrong. When the engine came ready for work the driver preparing it wanted to move it. He wound the engine into fore gear and opened the regulator. Mid clouds of steam the engine moved forward and then backward, shuddering at the half-turn of the wheels. When all the onlookers had finished gazing at it, the fitter was sent for to rectify his mistake. In the following panic he inadvertently worked on the wrong side; the result was the engine then went backwards in foregear and forwards in backgear. He took the lot down and started again. One probable reason for this type of mistake was that most Colwick men were accustomed

to GN engines, their valve gear was almost foolproof, the rods being shaped.

While on the subject of errors on these engines, the drive to the mechanical lubricators was from a return crank on the right driving wheel side rod crank pin. If this were put on the wrong angle, there was a broken lubricator at the first turn of the wheels.

In the 1946/7 period, we had a number of K2s at Colwick. Most of them were in a bad state due to the lack of general repairs. To use a local saying, they were 'held together with muck'. In spite of their poor condition, they did a lot of local passenger work. The first ten of these engines built had long slide bars. The rear ends of these bars were angled out to fit the connecting rod movement. The spectacle plate was fitted to the main frames between the leading coupled and driving wheels. This had an advantage for the fitters, as we were able to remove the crosshead for remetalling without disturbing the slidebars. When we had separated the piston and the crosshead, we just slid the crosshead to the rear and let it fall out of the wider space. The later engines had straight slide bars and the spectacle plate was shaped round the

leading coupled wheels. These engines had adjustable big ends with a cotter behind the brasses. In construction they were the same as Stirling's No 1 in York Museum.

Any vacuum cylinder trouble on K2s was a big job. The first thing we did was separate the engine and tender. The cylinders were in a mass of pipes, heater, vacuum and injector water and steam pipes. These were all under the drag box, under the cab floor. Most of the pipes had to be removed before we could get the vacuum cylinders down. On one engine (I believe it was 1726), we had to lower the trailing coupled wheels on the drop-pit to clear the cylinder trunnions from behind the wheel tyres. Fortunately, this job did not occur often. The leading coupled wheel brake blocks were up behind the cylinder castings. It was a lovely greasy job changing these. Small wonder the fitters working on K2s were known as the 'Black Gang'.

While the new Thurgoland Tunnel was being built between Sheffield and Manchester, much of the freight traffic between Colwick and Manchester was diverted via Egginton Junction and the Churnet Valley line to Macclesfield. For these duties we had a number of K2s

In workaday condition, K2 No. 61759 is seen at Boston on 23rd June 1958. The coal piled high in the tender was not of very good quality.

R. C. RILEY

transferred to Colwick. Among these was 1720 (old 1630). She had larger pony wheels than the other K2s and they came very close to the cylinder covers. She was the only K2 we had with steam sand ejectors on the leading coupled wheels, the others having dry sanders.

Some of the engines transferred had Westinghouse pumps and reservoirs fitted. This was a relic of their Great Eastern days. We also had 1729 with a side window cab, West Highland style. There was some class distinction on this engine as the fireman's side had a bucket seat. Due to the position of the reversing lever the driver had to be satisfied with a stool on the cab side.

The K2s were sent to Cowlairs Works for general repairs, and had often done a considerable mileage before we received them back at Colwick. On several occasions Colwick engines (and Boston's) were noted in Fort William. No. 1732 returned to us painted green; at that time Cowlairs appeared to be painting every engine green. We also had these engines working to Colwick from South Lynn. They were even in a worse state than ours, various parts were secured with signal wire. Several of the K2s finished their days as stationary boilers at various running sheds.

A number of B17s were in the area at that time. Those at Leicester GC and Woodford were generally sent to Colwick for repairs, valve and piston examinations and also lifting for axlebox examinations. This was rather peculiar as both Leicester and Woodford had lifting gear. Staff shortage was a possible explanation. These engines had a reputation for rough riding; the only seats provided in the cab were round piano stool type, held to the frames by three $\frac{1}{2}$ in studs at the base. These were constantly working loose. When they did, the seat swayed with the motion of the engine. At that period some of the cabs were loose on the frames as well, this adding to the general rough ride.

One of these engines, 1652, had experimental piston gland packing, three cast iron segments in a separate cast iron container, in the stuffing box. The whole fitted into the usual cylinder stuffing box. The usual method of assembling this was to stick the packing pieces on the piston rod with grease and build the casting round them. While on the subject of piston glands, the one on the middle engine could be interesting. To reach this, it was necessary to climb over the bogie basin casting. This casting had strengthening webs on top which formed places for water to settle. Generally there was a cocktail of water, oil, grease, and smoke box ash in these spaces. In taking the nuts off the gland cover, if the spanner slipped, you usually put your elbow in this mixture. All you could do, of course, was murmur 'How annoying', wipe your sleeve and carry on. Another way of doing this was to borrow the wind door off a J6 cab and put it across the three ponds; it did save a wetting.

The 2 to 1 arm of the Gresley valve gear was behind the cylinders on the B17s, and did not seem to wear as much as those in front of the cylinders. The middle valve had a very long spindle, but, unlike the K3s and A3s, it was possible to draw it out of the steam chest from the front of the engine. The regulator valve on 1647 was different to all the others we had. It was a small piston worked by the regulator handle in a casting on the 'J' pipe in the dome. To get at this for repairs or adjustment, it was necessary to remove the whole casting. Working on top of the boiler, lifting the casting out of the dome top, made one wonder if there were not

'Sandringhams' were quite often to be seen at King's Cross in the late 1930s, working from their home shed at Cambridge. This picture shows No. 2824 Lumley Castle *piloting an Ivatt Atlantic on what was probably the 5.00 p.m. from King's Cross, first stop Hitchin. There, the leading loco ran forward, the train engine took the first portion to Peterborough, and the pilot backed down on to the second portion and worked it to Cambridge.*

S. FREESE

Minor derailments were the bugbear of the operating staff. Here, J6 No. 3548 was off the rails at New Southgate. There was no shortage of labour to say what should be done, and how to do it.
COLLECTION
A. B. COLLINS

easier ways of earning a living. Rather a curious fact, the fitters at King's Cross called the 'J' pipe the 'Horse's Head'. Judging by the weight of these things in 1647's boiler, I think the horse must have been attached.

The crock of the B17s we had at that time was 1662. She was kept west of Colwick which meant Derby or Burton-on-Trent workings. The chopper finally came down when she dropped the middle big end while in Mapperley Tunnel and the driver kept her moving until he reached open air. She was hauled to Darlington Works after this incident. Darlington gradually overhauled all our B17s and turned them out in LNER green but with 'British Railways' painted in full on the tender. The only one I recollect with the hungry lion on the tender was 1664.

We had these engines working into Colwick from March, on the GE Section, and they had the small GE tenders. Some drivers who worked these engines on the return working were fearful about the water supply. There was no water crane between Colwick and Sleaford on the way to March, and doubt was always expressed as to whether there was enough water. As far as I know, there always was.

One evening, travelling home from Leicester Central Loco Depot, I was invited by the driver of the 5.20 pm to travel on the footplate with him. They

were Sheffield men (grinders). The engine was 1648 *Arsenal*. There was no question about the engine's ability to keep time — she was a flyer. As to the ride, Goose Fair had nothing like it! I'm convinced the trailing coupled wheels were running on the sleeper ends, not the rails.

Some of the B17s had drop grates in the fire box, and sometimes the ash-pit men left these in the open position. One Sunday afternoon one of the fire-lighters (steam-raisers), came on duty after sampling the products of John Barleycorn at the local pub, and consequently was a little dazed. He very carefully built a fire in the ash-pan and then realised his mistake; it was worth hearing. We gradually lost the B17s at Colwick when the B1s came along. They were transferred to the Eastern Counties, Norwich and March. The last one I had anything to do with was *Gunton*, but this was at King's Cross.

An engine that everybody seemed to like at Colwick was the J6, known to the old GN men in the depot as the 'A' engines. These engines were among the most trouble-free I have ever known. They ran on almost every job, from ballast workings to passenger trains. They were nearly always rostered for the Skegness and Mablethorpe excursions. We did not have any of the older type with inside sand boxes, but they did run in to us from Boston. These were known to us as the

'long fronts', due to the space on the foot-plate.

The valves and pistons on the J6s were simple and generally easy to remove and replace. The piston valve heads had four 5/16 in rings, 8 in diameter, or there-abouts, and I've known them to be $\frac{1}{4}$ in over size. On some of the engines the piston rings were square section, on others they were oblong, narrow edge to the cylinder bore. Here again there was often a variation in bore sizes. Removing the wheels from these engines was also a simple job. It was possible to remove the wheels, axleboxes, stays and springs as one unit. If this job were done on the drop-pit, there was nothing to it; if, however, we did it in the shop or on the shear legs, we had to detach the tender. These engines were all vacuum brake fitted. There were two cylinders in the rear of the frames, underneath the cab floor, and one under the tender. These gave very little trouble.

During 1948/9 we had the job of rigging some of the J6s with Whitaker tablet cat-chers for working over the M & GN line. There must have been a change of thought somewhere as a little later they were all taken off. Occasionally they did work to South Lynn, but this work was generally done by South Lynn K2s or J17s.

Potters Bar station would never be the same again after the widening work which can be seen here in its early stages on 21st August 1953, with Silver Link passing on the 1.48 p.m. arrival in King's Cross from Leeds.
D. A. DANT

THE BADGER'S BACK

MICHAEL JOYCE

IN the 1950s and 1960s I had got to know many footplatemen, particularly those in the Top Link at King's Cross, as a result of living in Hitchin, travelling to and from London regularly, and taking many photographs in that area. Wherever possible I obtained the names of the drivers and firemen concerned, and always sent to both of them enlargements of the photographs – something they were always delighted to receive. Before the coming of the diesels, where the engine crew are hidden behind a windscreen, one could easily recognise the driver or fireman, even if the steam engine were travelling at speed, and I soon discovered that the crews treasured such photographs even more than those taken at a platform. A warm, friendly relationship developed with many crews who were always ready to talk and, where no great risk to themselves was involved, to offer unofficial rides with them on the footplate.

Most of my trips were short – between Hitchin and King's Cross in either direction – but as my work made it necessary to travel further afield on occasions, sometimes I was able to make much longer trips. So it was one late May morning at Newcastle Central station in the early 1960s. I had come over from Norway by sea and the coaches of the boat train were attached to a morning express for King's Cross. There was time for me to walk up to the head of the train after our coaches had been coupled up, and I was pleased to see a King's Cross A4 at the head. It was 60028 *Walter K. Whigham*, complete with corridor tender.

Surprisingly, 60028 looked a sorry sight! One was so used to seeing King's Cross Pacifics spotlessly clean that it came as a shock to see the dirty sides of a Top Link engine – one that was often used for the non-stop 'Elizabethan' during the summer season. My surprise at viewing this rather

depressing sight was soon forgotten when I found that its driver was Charlie Price – one of the King's Cross Top Link of the period that also included such well-known names as Hoole, Hailstone, Turner etc. Charlie Price lived at Hatfield, and many were the times we had travelled together in a train when he was either going on duty or going home, and we were very good friends.

Discovering that I was travelling in the train, an invitation to ride with him and his fireman (Colin) was soon forthcoming, and accepted. I was told to wait in the train until we had crossed the bridge out of the station, and then come through the corridor tender on to the footplate. Charlie would arrange with the guard to ensure that the corridor connection from the train would be left open, and there would be no trouble from that department!

A4 No. 60034 on the 'Capitals Limited' passing B1 No. 61203 on an outer suburban train, outside Potters Bar station on 21st September 1949. The Pacific was named Lord Faringdon, *after the one-time Chairman of the Great Central Railway, who, at the grouping, became Deputy Chairman of the LNER.*

D. A. DANT

No. 60003 passing Wymondley on an up express in 1953. This may have been a Sunday service, the engine working up to King's Cross and carrying the reversed headboard of one of the following day's premier trains. The engine was named Andrew K. McCosh, *after the Chairman of the LNER Locomotive Committee for many years, and who was closely concerned with Gresley's locomotive proposals.* G. W. GOSLIN

I went back to my compartment to tell my travelling companions that I had not missed the train but that they should not worry if they did not see me for some time. I did not tell them where I was going in case an injudicious word might be dropped to a travelling ticket collector on his rounds that would subsequently cause trouble for my footplate friends.

We left Newcastle on time and, as we slowly moved over the bridge, I made my way down the train and into the brake van next to the engine. Much to my surprise, I found not only the guard but Colin, the fireman, sitting in the guard's seat! There was a simple explanation for his absence from the footplate. It appeared that, at the last moment before departure, a driver from Sunderland, who wanted to learn the road from Newcastle to York, offered to fire the Pacific to give Colin an unexpected but welcome break. Colin seemed to be very pleased about this – exceptionally so – but it was not until I arrived on the footplate that I learned the reasons!

My passage through the corridor tender was not without its problems. It was narrow, and with the engine being very dirty, the small spectacle glass at the rear of the corridor prevented any light getting through, and as it was normal practice for the corridor to be used as a depository for the long shovel and slice, and the latter being twisted from many explorations in the intense heat of the firebox, I stumbled and nearly crawled my way on to the footplate.

The Sunderland driver-cum-fireman was startled to see a 'civilian' emerge from the tender, but Charlie Price at the regulator soon set his mind at rest, and I was invited to take the fireman's seat on the right-hand side of the cab. This proved to be another example of an engine ready for a visit to Doncaster for it had a large tear across the seat, and most of the stuffing had long since gone, but that was the least of my problems.

Long-serving members of our Society may recall an article of mine in the May 1966 edition of the 'G.O.' when I described a run on the footplate of 60067 *Ladas*. On that occasion, the engine had not been long out of Plant, and its riding was as smooth as anyone could expect from an engine at speed. *Walter K. Whigham* was right at the other end of the scale! To quote an expression often used by driver Charlie Price – 'It was as rough as a badger's back'.

I could hardly stand up on the footplate as I made my way across to the fireman's seat. The engine literally bounced and bucked, violently swinging from side to side, without any semblance of rhythm. Coal littered the footplate. Large lumps and small, the latter skittering about, and some soon found their way under the flaps, flying to the permanent way.

The volunteer fireman from Sunderland heaved over a massive piece of coal and placed it under my feet so that at least I had something on which to place my feet and, he hoped, brace myself against the

vicious thrashing that never stopped. I soon found that I had to lift my left leg outwards and upwards and force my foot against the back of the firebox to have any chance of staying in my seat. I hung on to the rail outside the cab window with my right hand, but even this did not prevent my being banged and bashed against the cab side! This was a Gresley Pacific at its most evil!

Dirty and violent 60028 might have been, but it could still steam well. Charlie Price was one of the 'full regulator' brigade; he liked to drive fast and hard, and the engine was responding well. There was not a great deal of opportunity for high speed between Newcastle and Darlington, the first stop, but even so the fireman had his hands full to maintain a good head of steam.

I felt very sorry for him, and it became crystal clear why Charlie's regular fireman was only too happy to be sitting in the brake van! Our friend from Sunderland had never fired a Gresley Pacific before, with its large firebox, and the technique of having a fire that was thin in the centre and heavy at the corners. Add to that a driver who used the regulator fully open, and a footplate that rose, dropped, swayed and swung in a mad, malicious dance, making it nearly impossible to get a shovelful of coal through the firehole, never mind put them in the right places. He was not a happy man! How he must have regretted his generous offer to a fellow footplateman. As we slowly steamed into

Darlington, he collected his coat from the locker and made it clear that he was leaving. He'd had enough. He would find another way to learn the road to York!

Colin rejoined us during the stop and cleared up some of the mess on the footplate. Despite his problems, the Sunderland man had left a good head of steam in the boiler, but the fire needed some attention and Colin soon got to work.

Now we set off for the dash across the Plain of York, and there was a fairly fast timing to maintain. *Walter* had lost none of his exuberance during the short stop at Darlington, and we crabbed and crashed on our merry way. Colin, with his considerable experience of Pacific firing, fared much better than his predecessor but nevertheless even he didn't get every shovelful into the box!

I was feeling sore and sorry for myself, but found that there was still excitement and enjoyment in the experience. I would be leaving the train at York for I was going on to Leeds before I finally returned home to Hitchin. We sped across the flat land in great style until just before Tollerton we ran into a series of signal checks. We were never brought to a standstill, but Charlie Price offered the opinion that we were being 'timed' by signalmen and Control, and from then onwards he drove a little more circumspectly.

By then it was time for me to leave the footplate so that I might have the opportunity to have a quick wash, collect my luggage from my compartment and leave the train at York. Another 'commando course' through the tender and I was back on firm ground again – or, at least, that is what the riding of the brake van seemed after the eruptions on the footplate!

I bore bruises on my ribs for some days after my ride, but the trip has always been treasured in my memory. It served to show that even Top Link Gresley Pacifics were not always the smooth and perfect riders so eloquently described by well-known railway authors who, having obtained a footplate pass, probably enjoyed an engine carefully selected by the shed staff. That is not a criticism of the writers – they could only report on their own experiences – but rather a recognition that even the best can have their 'off days' and that footplatemen, in their day-to-day work, had to take what they were given and make the best of it.

No. 60006 was named Sir Ralph Wedgwood, *after the LNER's Chief General Manager who retired in 1938. He came from the North Eastern Railway at grouping and, although Gresley's superior, the two men were on friendly terms, and only occasionally do the records indicate serious disagreement between them. The train was the 5.00 p.m. down Newcastle, climbing to Potters Bar on 31st July 1952.*   D. A. DANT

Ivatt fitted a larger, domed boiler to the basic Stirling design of shunting tank, and LNER J52 class No. 4252 was one of twenty turned out from Doncaster in 1901/2.
GRESLEY SOCIETY COLLECTION

SOME LNER TANK ENGINES
SHUNTING ENGINES AT COLWICK

SID CHECKLEY

THE type of engine at Colwick that did the most work and got the least attention was the shunting engine. There were J50s, J52s and the odd N5. Mainly they went to work in the early hours of Monday morning and came in the shed at odd times during the week for coal. Often they only had repairs carried out when the driver threatened, 'I'm not taking it out until it's repaired!' The common trouble with the J52s was joints blowing, chiefly piston glands and cylinder covers, the reason being that they were grossly overloaded. The steam chest spindle glands blew almost continually. These engines were badly worn in the steam chest and usually the weight of the valve buckle was on the spindle packing. Some of this was what was known as 'soft packing'. This was a type of hemp in a graphite impregnated skin which was held in position by a cover over the stuffing box, in turn held by two nuts on studs. The usual thing (if you could get away with it) was to fill the box with packing soaked in thick oil. Care had to be taken though, because if it was too solid it was impossible to move the reversing lever.

Some of the J52s had metallic packing which was held in place in a box by a spring inside the stuffing box. In time these packings wore sharp edges, and some were like razor blades. Occasionally, heavier repairs were carried out on these engines, and renewing slide valves was an interesting job. They generally ran until they 'blew through'. That is to say they wore until they were so thin a detector hole bored in the valve face allowed steam to blow through from the live steam to the cylinders. The valves were 'yellow metal' and the job was to fit them to the buckle and the steam chest faces. The usual thing was to fit them in pairs. The piston rings lasted an amazing length of time, and a roar up the chimney was generally the first indication that anything was wrong. On examination the rings were generally found in about a dozen pieces.

Lubrication of the J52s was by means of a sight feed lubricator fixed on the cab side, inside the cab on the fireman's side. The axleboxes were oiled by a worsted trimming in each axlebox top in an oil well in the box top. Sometimes these engines ran hot axleboxes. This meant removing the wheels to remetal the axlebox, usually a straightforward job. The trailing wheels on some of the J52s could be interesting. On the 'top springers', the trailing wheel springs were in a cast iron box arranged across the frame. This enclosed a series of coil springs. If this was not fastened up before lifting, when the engine was lifted, the box separated and there was a cascade of springs into the pit. Putting them back was an acrobat's job, and one needed about four hands. Much 'running shed Esperanto' was heard when this happened. Most of the J52s had bearing springs underneath the axleboxes and with these there was no difficulty as it was possible to roll out the wheels, springs and frame stays as a unit.

These engines all had saddle tanks. The disadvantage was that if the boilersmiths had to get at any of the boiler stays in the firebox crown, the tank had to come off the boiler. With the engine in the shop underneath the overhead crane this was a straightforward job, or was it? The first thing was to empty the water out of the tank. This was accomplished by removing a plug in the equalising pipe under the boiler. Often a little water came out and the pipe became blocked with dirt, and sometimes this was not noticed. To disconnect the various holding-down bolts in the tank, it was the practice for an apprentice (a slim one) to get inside the tank with spanners and hold the bolt heads. The method of entry was to push his legs through the filler hole and down the tank side inside. If, when lowering himself inside the tank, you saw the expression on his face change, you realized the tank was not empty, he had put his feet in the remaining water, the equaliser pipe *was* blocked! I have seen many tanks removed from these engines and it is surprising how many times this has happened. As an aside, although it was a squeeze getting into the tanks, it was surprising how much room there was once inside.

At odd times these engines were in collision in the shunting yards, but they never seemed to sustain much damage. Right up to the end of their days, some of them carried wooden buffer beams. These were made of hard wood sandwiched between steel plates.

The J52s performed shunting in Colwick Yard and district, and I believe there were seven jobs. Two were to be found in the goods yard at Nottingham London Road

The characteristic Great Northern saddle tank was originated by Stirling and continued by Ivatt. This example, J52 class No. 68877, was built at Doncaster in 1905, and is seen shunting at Grantham c.1952.
JOHN F. CLAY

87

Gresley enlarged the dimensions of Ivatt's shunting engine, and replaced the saddle tank by side tanks. These were extended to the front of the engine, but with sloping front ends to aid visibility, and provision was made for access to the motion. This picture shows J50 No. 68975 at Colwick in July 1958. RAS MARKETING (PHOTOMATIC)

Low Level, one of which was a tripper, that is to say it worked trains between Low Level Yard and Colwick. Some of these trains came through the exchange sidings at Nottingham London Road where traffic was exchanged with the ex-LMS. One of the engines was at Derby Friargate for local shunting and came back to Colwick for boiler wash-outs. It was a representative of the class which ran away from the coal stage at Slack Lane, down into the depot and demolished the lavatories at the bottom of the shed. Fortunately, no one was in the building at the time.

We had various J50s. They seemed to come and go, though the regular resident was 68981. For a long time this was the 'Loco Pilot', worked by two shifts of men in the day time, and worked round the depot all day. Its only excursion into the distance was to deliver wagons of ashes to the Civil Engineer's Depot, and to shunt wagons in the Private Repairers' sidings. As there were only two drivers on this engine, it was usually well looked after.

A curious job was to renew the weight bar spring. The 'weight bar' was the shaft across the engine that worked the links from the reversing rod (sorry, bridle rod). The links were balanced by a coil spring on this shaft, and the easiest way to change the spring was to take the shaft out from the engine. The shaft was on top of the motion and, to get at it, one went through the access holes in the side tanks. When the bearing caps were removed, the fitter at one end and his assistant at the other, lifted, pushed, and muttered remarks about design staff, and drew the shaft over the frame and lowered it to the floor. It

Examples of Thomas Parker's 0–6–2T design for the MS&L were to pass through Sid Checkley's hands at Colwick. Here, N5 class No. 69309 (built by Beyer Peacock in 1898) was photographed working a local freight train at Louth, sometime in the 1950s. It was not to be withdrawn until 1960. JOHN F. CLAY

was a weighty article, and putting it back was the worst part of the job. With engines having the shaft underneath the motion it was a simple task. The shaft was dropped on the brake rods, the remnants of the broken spring removed, a new one placed on the shaft, and lifted back into position.

The earlier members of the class had adjustable small end brasses, an old GN feature. These were adjusted with a wedge-shaped block with an adjusting screw through it. When this reached the limit, the brasses were removed, reduced on the faces, and a distance shim was inserted between the wedge and the brasses. As a result, the small end lasted a

very long time. In later representatives the small ends had plain bushes.

The J50s were commonly known as 'Ardsley Tanks' but they were also known as 'Long Tanks' and 'Ally Slopers'.

The N5 tanks were used occasionally at Colwick for various shunting jobs, but were not popular on this work as they were vacuum-braked with only one vacuum cylinder. Many of these engines had a different type of brake block from the other ex-LNER classes. This fitted in a slot in the brake hanger with the usual pin through a hole in the block. Something unusual was the use of snap-headed rivets on the tank and bunker sides. Really they were a link with the old MS & LR.

N2 FOOTPLATE MEMORIES

BERT COLLINS

WHEN I submitted some notes to our Editor on the experiences I encountered with my first trip on a V2, he very kindly suggested that members might show interest in some further scribblings. In pondering the idea, the thought occurred that very little had been featured in the 'G.O.' over the years on the one subject that was probably nearest to the society – namely N2s.

As I explained in my previous piece, my career on the footplate was quite short but nonetheless interesting. During the period 1947–1956 I managed to work on every N2 to be stationed at either Top Shed, Hornsey or Hatfield. This represented over 75% of the entire class! Whilst I would be the first to admit that this did not make me an expert on the subject, it did, however, provide me with an insight into a well-known class of loco-

motive that other enthusiasts would not necessarily be aware of. For instance, I still have vivid memories of the layout of the footplate of certain members of the class which varied from engine to engine, and also of whether the engine was a good steamer or not.

I encountered members of the class on my very first day as a cleaner on 26th August 1947. Our chargehand informed us that our day's work would involve the cleaning of two 'Big Mets' – as the N2s were known – together with one of the new Thompson Pacifics which were then being rostered to work the 'Yorkshire Pullman'.

We were given a pan of paraffin, some cotton waste, ladders and scrapers. Two N2s were parked in the 'Shed' road of the tank shed, having their boilers washed, together with a routine brake exam-

ination. In the post-war malaise, engines were sadly neglected, both externally and mechanically, and I am afraid our efforts as cleaners did little to help. All we seemed to do was to smear the dirt from one part to another and leave it looking worse than it did when we started! Some drivers who were beginning to receive regular engines on a two-shift basis, and keeping them clean themselves, forbade the chargehand to allow us near their engines when they were 'Shed'. Things did improve, however, as those who remember the 1948 locomotive exchanges will, I hope, bear witness – we were responsible for cleaning all the exchange engines.

During our few months as cleaners, we were encouraged to help locomotivemen with their engine preparation with a view to us gaining knowledge of footplate procedures. I always enjoyed being allowed to

Ivatt's N1 class 0–6–2T, and Gresley's improved version, the N2, were a familiar sight at King's Cross for fifty years. This picture shows N2 No. 4757 and N1 No. 4576 resting between duties in what was known as 'No. 9 carriage road', which became Platform No. 8 after widening in 1938.

S. FREESE

The classic GN suburban picture in LNER and early BR days: an N2 and an eight-coach train made up of two quadruple articulated sets. Bert Collins' first engine, No. 69535, is shown working hard on the 4.51 p.m. King's Cross to Hatfield, north of Potters Bar on 2nd June 1951. The 'main line' destination board signified anywhere from New Barnet northwards.

G. W. GOSLIN

make up the back corners on main line engines as they were being prepared in front of the main line shed. I hoped that this would give me a chance to gain useful experience with the shovel. These hopes were later to be dashed as I took my practical firing test. But more of this later.

On attaining the age of 16, I was informed that I was going to spend two weeks on the footplate preparatory to taking my test as a passed cleaner (spare fireman). I was to report to Driver Dick Hunt on engine No 9535 at King's Cross station. This engine was commendably clean on the outside and positively gleamed on the footplate, with all its brass and copperwork burnished to gold standard, a credit to both driver and fireman. Dick was a leading member of King's Cross Mutual Improvement Class and he undertook to give instruction to all cleaners before they took their tests. I spent two happy weeks trying to learn the method of flicking coal through the narrow trap of the GN type firehole door with a success rate of about two shovelsful in every five! I also helped with cleaning the engine and learned that a few white sponge cloths presented to the signalman at Broad Street would yield a tin of cream metal polish which brought 9535's brightwork to a brilliant finish in very short order. As we

More specifically bearing a 'Hatfield' destination board, No. 69591 leaving Potters Bar, signalled for the slow road on to Brookmans Park, on 3rd August 1953. This was the loco on which Bert Collins passed his fireman's test.
D. A. DANT

steamed through the countryside of Hertfordshire and Middlesex, Dick would fire the odd question to me on the dreaded rule book, just to see if I had been swotting up! The crunch came when it was time for me to take the test to qualify me as a passed cleaner.

One morning, I was summoned to the Top Shed office of Inspector Mitchell for the examination. His dingy office was surrounded by faded sepia photographs of 'Atlantics' and 'Pacifics', each signed by its designer. I spent the morning undergoing written and oral tests on the rule book and the well known 'black' book which described locomotive management techniques for enginemen. Mr Mitchell informed me that I had passed these tests satisfactorily and that it was time for my practical test on a suburban train.

Following the advent of the N2s, Ivatt's C12 class 4–4–2T left King's Cross for more remote areas. However, in the later 1930s, No. 4511 was allocated to Hitchin shed for branch line duties; it would be interesting to learn how it found its way back to King's Cross. N2 No. 4749 can be seen in the background with an 'Alexandra Palace' destination board, ready for its next duty.
S. FREESE

'How good are you with the shovel, lad?' enquired Mr Mitchell.

'Not too bad Sir, although I am hopeless at trying to fire left-handed.'

'Well, walk down to the Suburban Station, Platform 13, where Inspector Manyard will be waiting with the 1.54pm Hatfield. Introduce yourself to him and the driver of the engine where you will take your test. Incidentally the engine is 9591 – a left-hander!'

At this point, it would be as well to explain the footplate arrangements on N2s. Obviously, several members will have seen the footplate on the Society's N2 at Loughborough, but this differs somewhat from the original arrangement in that when in traffic the driver's 'platform' stood some six inches higher than the firing 'well' and was extended level to the right-hand edge of the firehole door, rather than the lower position as at present. To the rear of this edge, a curve was cut in the driver's platform – just under the water test tap – so that a bucket could be accommodated. On the fireman's side, the floor was raised slightly to just level with, and the length of, the cab door, whilst the platform area surrounding the handbrake column stood some nine inches high, to be level with the top edge of the splasher that projected from the rear of the front tank. With four varying floor heights, the only area available for standing while firing was some 2 ft 6 in wide by the length of bunker to firehole door. There was little trouble for the naturally right-handed person firing on GN-built locomotives, but all LNER engines were built for left-hand drive, and the only way to fire a left-hander was left-handed, bearing in mind that the footplate layout was a mirror image of the GN-built engine.

OK! It is quite possible for a right-handed person to shovel left-handed, but when coal has to be placed precisely on the firebox grate via the well known GN firehold trap, problems arise!

Back then to 9591. The rostered fireman had informed me that he had made the fire up, and that a little sprinkle of coal around the box, as the train entered Gasworks Tunnel, should see me to Finsbury Park. As I was on test, my movements had to comply with the rule book and the 'black' book – as far as my memory would allow! This certainly precluded the over-emission of smoke at the front end, as well as me being responsible for checking the train as we left, to ensure that all

was well and that all carriage doors were closed. There were other procedures which needed the fireman's attention as well as raising steam and water in the boiler – for instance keeping a watchful eye on the road ahead, and complying with any instructions that the driver might give.

I have previously described how I found it difficult to find the firehole door trap when shovelling right-handed. I found it almost impossible when firing left-handed! As we churned our way through Gasworks and Copenhagen Tunnels, I struggled to get any amount of coal through the trap that I could, in the hope that something would happen. Luckily for me it did. No 9591 turned out to be an excellent steamer and I was able to set the trap on the firehole door latch at such an angle as to allow sufficient air into the firebox, and thus keep down the emission of too much smoke caused by my being unable to arrange the fire in the grate precisely as I would have liked.

Meanwhile, Inspector Manyard and Driver Bloggs stoically maintained their

position on the driver's platform while I paddled ankle deep in misdirected lumps of Blidworth hard! Despite all this preceding mayhem, we arrived at Finsbury Park with safety valves simmering and with three-quarters of a glass of water showing in the boiler. Perfect! I was now able to sweep up and keep the floor tidy. The thought of glancing over to the driver and inspector was terrifying but I could feel sure what they were thinking. The run from Finsbury Park to Oakleigh Park proved reasonably successful as Mr Manyard dismounted and made his way home, and the rostered fireman rejoined the engine. The driver beckoned me over to his side and informed me that when we reached New Barnet I could book off. At least I think he said book off!

My efforts in front of Inspector Manyard must have proved adequate as I soon found myself rostered through the shed duty and yard shunting links in quick succession. In the shed duty link one would often be rostered to cover a spare turn from a higher link, and it happened that on one

A winter midday at King's Cross suburban station in BR days, with the 12.30 p.m. all stations to Hertford North about to leave.
EDITOR'S COLLECTION

No. 69535 again, now ready to leave Platform 4 at King's Cross with an empty stock working, on 23rd September 1960. Until renumbering in recent years there was no Platform 3, which, until 1934, was a bay inserted in No. 4. R. F. ORPWOOD

or two occasions I found myself on running turns. The first was a two Hertford return diagram – happily on a right-handed engine – my first full running job. I informed the driver of my inexperience and he kindly suggested that if I looked after the stoking he would work the injectors. Our engine turned out to be a good steamer and I was able to enjoy a fairly pleasant evening with my first solo run as a fledgling fireman.

We were also sometimes booked passenger shunt pilot at King's Cross. This was the thin end of the wedge as far as N2s were concerned. Unlike some principal stations down the line who enjoyed specially prepared engines for pilot duty, King's Cross usually employed badly run-down N2s as passenger pilots as a way of seeing their mileage out before visiting the works for overhaul. This was all right if we were pottering around the Milk Yard or taking vehicles off incoming trains and placing them in Platform 1 for unloading, but when it came to lifting a train of odd stock from King's Cross to Holloway or Waterworks Sidings at Wood Green, these old rattle-traps were never quite up to the job and it became a bit of a scramble to get the train clear of main running lines to avoid causing delay to other traffic.

Eventually, I joined Joe Holland in the 'Odd Met' link, where most of our N2

work involved freight trips to Alexandra Palace, Edgware and High Barnet, as well as the odd passenger and empty stock turns that were unsuitable for rostering in the regular 'Met' link.

It was fortuitous for me that I was able to travel the old GN 'Northern Heights' branches from the footplate before they all closed. Most diagrams in the 'Odd Met' link involved the working of coal and goods trains from Highbury Vale (adjacent to where the Arsenal football stadium can be seen) to various depots on the branches. The load from Highbury Vale was as little as 12 coal wagons loaded plus brake van or its equivalent. This may seem small beer for an engine as burly as an N2, but from Highbury Vale gradients as steep as 1 in 60 against the engine made the climb to Highgate quite difficult. We would back the train out of Highbury Vale. In the meantime, it would be necessary for me to make up a thickish fire, with the back corners made right up and to keep the boiler well filled with water. Most times we would take the train to Finsbury Park where a respite would be allowed so that the boiler could be topped up in readiness for the climb past Finsbury Park No 7 Box and up to Stroud Green and Crouch End. With an 'Odd Met' engine, it was a good bet that its performance would not be 100% and it was usual to be fighting for

steam by Crouch End, so that the full boiler of water at Finsbury Park allowed us the luxury of not needing to use the injectors for a good part of the way to Highgate. However, if steam *was* in short supply, we would not use the injectors at all and things could be quite hairy as we entered the first of the two Highgate tunnels. Joe Holland and I would stoop down and mask our faces against the exhaust fumes as the engine struggled in the tunnel. A watchful eye would have to be kept on the gauge glasses to make sure that water was at least visible above the bottom nut. If not, jump! Luckily, such drastic steps were never necessary, although if we were bound for High Barnet or Edgware, the heavy fire that remained to get us to Highgate resulted in the engine blowing off for much of the rest of the journey – to the obvious annoyance of many of the local residents.

In 1948 there were at least two turns to Edgware. As the train left Mill Hill East along the single line to Edgware, it was as if the railway was stuck in a time capsule.

Although the station had lost its passenger traffic with the introduction of the tube services on the new Northern Line extension, Edgware station remained solidly Great Northern. A permanent staff of shunters and goods porters were employed for the distribution and allo-

No. 69498 with a Hertford North train at Palmers Green in 1956. The new BR standard non-corridor stock which had replaced the Gresley articulated sets, whilst more comfortable, offered less accommodation, so there were complaints of overcrowding in the rush hours.   J. VENN

cation of the goods that we had brought and these were distributed to the surrounding areas. Whilst at Edgware, we would have to carry out any shunting duties required. This applied also to the various other stations on the north London branches that still possessed goods yards.

Passenger train workings in the 'Odd Met' link could also be troublesome with the engines available to us. Many of these engines were run down and still fitted with Gresley's Twin Tube superheater – not one of the great man's most successful designs. Constant problems with steam and water, particularly on down workings, sometimes made life awkward, although, with experience, I was beginning to master the technique of shovelling left-handed.

One engine, 9545, was the last condenser engine in the London area to be fitted with GN-pattern Ramsbottom safety valves – of interest from an enthusiast's point of view, but it did not help that she started to simmer at the valves at 140 psi and blow off at 150! If one were coupled to one of the heavier 1929-built 'Quad-Art' sets, the northbound trip would be a struggle with the shortfall of pressure, although 9545 was a good steamer. However, there was no problem on the up journey as most of the time 130

psi was all that we usually required, due to the long sections between stations where the engine coasted downhill and the boiler could make too much steam if we were not careful, resulting in that nasty surge at the safety valves as the train stopped sharply in the station. Many will remember the soaking they received as the valves lifted, spraying water all over the platform. As a rule this was due either to the over-zealous efforts of the fireman or to an uncontrollable free-steaming boiler. On the other hand, occasionally we would be allowed the luxury of a trip on an engine from the regular 'Met' link which would mean a nice clean engine, plenty of steam and a good ride!

Some of the later left-hand N2s were equipped with a pull-out type of steam cock for the injectors rather than the familiar brass wheel and handle type. This helped the fireman considerably when working tightly-timed peak hour services, and it seems a pity that the idea was not adopted universally – probably because of the old enemy, cost. The only other class that I found to be fitted with this device was the B1 and this for the live steam injector only. It was also of interest to me to note that all the N2s so fitted were at King's Cross, and all were in the regular 'Met' link!

Late in 1948, I moved to Hornsey where I was soon rostered into Hornsey's No 6 Local Goods and South London Link.

The first thing to say about Hornsey's N2s at that time, apart from the few engines in the regular 'Met' link, was that they were not choice examples of the class. Four engines, Nos 9560/1/6/7 were all positively rogue! This itinerant quartet had spent their existences on the LNER, travelling around the system, where they must have found disfavour wherever they went. Indeed, 9567 (as LNER 897) seemed to be the gipsy of the entire class, finding itself shipped to Scotland, East Anglia, the Midlands and anywhere else that would give the thing room and board, presumably until the engine's shortcomings were discovered. It seemed that Hornsey was the final resting place as far as these villains were concerned, as they drifted there from other depots to spend most of their last days at Hornsey in general, and, with their unwilling hosts in No 6 Link in particular, they were relegated to empty coach and local goods work only. For a start, they were fitted with Detroit hydrostatic lubricators, which to me was never the best form of cylinder and valve lubrication. Most of the N2 class were fitted with Wakefield mechanical lubricators which required the minimum of attention from the engine crew other than topping up, whereas the Detroit required a quite complicated procedure by the fireman to replenish the lubricator before leaving the shed. The Detroit was also a bulky device that was fitted directly over the fireman's seat, on an already cramped footplate layout, and which resulted in the fireman's seat becoming smothered with a mucky mixture of oil and water. The seat, being attached to the handbrake column by brackets, could thus be used only when swivelled round in front of the fireman's cabside door. This arrangement in turn impeded the fireman's backswing when shovelling and could often result in a nasty rap on the knuckles. Having tried to overcome this problem, it was then necessary to try and raise some steam. All four of these engines were poor steamers and rattled and banged while running. Small wonder then that a minor revolt occurred when many drivers refused point blank to take them on any passenger workings, although as N2s, the authorities were perfectly justified in rostering them on non-Metropolitan passenger duties.

It was on one of these engines that I was to witness mass hysteria at King's Cross station when the pop singer, Johnnie Ray, who had just completed a stint on the TV programme 'Sunday Night at the London Palladium', was known to be travelling on the overnight sleeper to Scotland which departed from the then Platform 8 while we stood behind some coaches on Platform 7. Every vantage point available was occupied by young girls hoping to get a glimpse of their idol. When he finally appeared, the whole of King's Cross station was treated to a crescendo of squealing and adulation the like of which it is doubtful that King's Cross has seen before or since. I was with a young passed fireman, Kenny Hempstead, and our interest centred not on the subject of all this hysteria but on those who were perpetrating it, whilst our hapless N2 acted as a more than adequate crash barrier!

Hornsey provided accommodation for the other N2 waifs and strays such as 9522 – 'The Green Goddess' as she was nicknamed at Hornsey – although by the time we received her from Neasden her lovely green livery had become sadly begrimed. It seems a pity that Neasden should have been allocated this engine in the first place as both King's Cross and Hornsey men would have delighted in keeping her clean had they been given the chance.

N2 No. 69567 at Doncaster in 1949, fresh from overhaul and repainting in BR lined black livery. Most of the class were built by contractors, but this was one of a small batch of six turned out by Doncaster in 1925. Allocated to Hornsey at the time, it was not fitted with condensing apparatus, so could not be used on the underground lines to Moorgate. This loco was not one of Bert Collins' favourites.
JOHN F. CLAY

Among other non-condenser types we had engines such as 9505, 9519 and 69594. No 9505 was probably the last member of the class in London to retain her LNER livery. It was suggested that there was a slightly loose tyre on one of the coupled drivers, and so she had to spend her time at Waterworks Sidings at Wood Green. This meant that the engine took a considerable time to see her mileage out before she visited shops for general overhaul and correction to the wheels – if indeed this was the fault. No 69594 was by far the best of the non-condensers and it was not surprising that she was to be found on Hornsey's diagram to Luton which involved a return with upwards of 40 wagons loaded with Vauxhall/Bedford vehicles crated for export. These were all marshalled at the purpose-built sidings at Oakleigh Park. The Luton diagram entailed a morning signing on and a small goods train working to Hatfield where we disposed of the train, filled the tank, and this left us sufficient time to have our breakfast. We then made up our Luton branch train and awaited train time. At this period (1950s) Hatfield was a thriving little goods yard that sometimes sported two pilots (usually ex-GER 0–6–0Ts) and with workings to various places in the area that were operated from Hatfield. Our train would proceed to Ayot St Lawrence which at that time still had passing places and where we awaited the arrival of an up passenger train. One driver would dismount and take a quick stroll into the nearby fields where he would exercise his 12-bore shot gun.

When we left Ayot, our route took us 'over the hills and far away', as it was known, to Luton Bute Street, where one could catch a glimpse of the Midland main line. Our train of cars was marshalled and we would make our way back to Oakleigh Park, stopping briefly at Hatfield for water. The Luton turn was always one of my favourite jobs with an N2 and, as I have suggested earlier, 69594 was by far the best of the 'Odd' engines at Hornsey and was always kept, as far as possible, for this duty. She would then sometimes be rostered in the evening on a two-trip King's Cross–Hertford passenger diagram, giving 69594 a good day's work.

In 1954 I joined Driver Bob London for a short spell in Hornsey's Met Link where my regular engine was 69531. I say a short spell as Bob was soon to leave me and join the Main Line link. I was then rostered with Driver Bert Sims. Bert was one of the most likeable characters that I ever met on the railway. He was Branch Secretary of ASLEF and although nowadays such a disclosure would possibly be met with some scorn by the ill-informed, Bert was a warm and humorous person who did a great deal to promote a good spirit at Hornsey. I enjoyed every moment that I worked with Bert and 69531. My first meeting with 69531, however, was not the best in that her previous crews had not afforded her the care that such a good engine deserved. She had recently acquired a boiler fitted with a Robinson superheater which meant that there were no problems with regard to steam. Moreover, her front end must have been set perfectly as she was by far the strongest member of the class that I ever worked on and Bert Sims exploited this to the full. Even drivers from Top Shed grudgingly admitted their envy at times when they would enjoy a ride home 'on the cushions' and experienced her swift 'turn of foot' as she made light of even the heaviest of twin 'Quad-Art' sets.

Over a period of a week or two, I managed to get the footplate of 69531 into some semblance of order, and some polish on her copper and brasswork. At first, Bert showed little enthusiasm for over-zealous cleaning, but once he had appreciated that he had found himself rostered with a particularly good engine, he could be found underneath the engine cleaning the valve gear (a rare sight for a driver!) whilst I did my best to make her look presentable externally.

During the morning and evening peak periods, trains would leave Finsbury Park simultaneously, and, almost without exception, 69531 would be the winner. On one particular morning diagram we were booked to Moorgate, slow line, while a King's Cross train left on the main

line. It was always of interest to passengers to see who would win. It would be immodest of me to harp on this, but the Top Shed crew on the other train were always to be seen with glum faces! To be fair to the King's Cross crew, their train was almost certain to be checked at Belle Isle. The start from Finsbury Park was almost always simultaneous – unlike the situation we see today on BR, whereby one train will be sent on its way just as another is entering an adjoining platform! As we left Finsbury Park, it would be full throttle past East Goods Yard and on to Holloway. From here we would be coasting down the bank as the two trains splayed out on the tracks where the old GN station stood, coming together just north of Caledonian Road bridge. This little interlude was enjoyed by a number of the passengers, and those who travelled in the front brake of the 'Quad-Art' when the train was full could catch a glimpse of their engine at full snort!

By now, 69531 was the equal of any N2 in the London suburban links, and this was due in no small measure to the two regular drivers who often did little maintenance jobs themselves on the engine, as well as

badgering the fitting and boiler staff to keep the engine in good fettle. It was a pity, therefore, that as soon as she was due for overhaul, she had to visit Stratford Works. Her previous overhaul and repaint had been carried out at Doncaster where she also received the most beautifully forged and machined GN-type regulator handle that I ever saw. It was always a joy to keep this well burnished.

On return from Stratford, not only was this handle replaced by a very crude affair, but, instead of the nice lined livery that she had enjoyed previously, Stratford saw fit to 'adorn' her in their notorious 'Tar and Feather' finish, leaving her looking a forlorn shadow of her old self. Although the two drivers protested to the authorities, nothing was done and the enthusiasm that existed before she went away was never quite the same after she returned.

It seemed to me fitting, therefore, that when Mainline introduced their N2 model, the BR lined livery version was 69531. My own model serves as a personal tribute to an engine that gave me great personal pleasure to work on.

In its latter days, No. 896, when renumbered 69566, was another of the 'rogue quartet' of N2s. It was fitted with the taller chimney and left-hand drive. The Pacific in the background was Robert the Devil.

S. FREESE

MEMORIES OF THE KING'S CROSS N2s

F. G. FOWLER

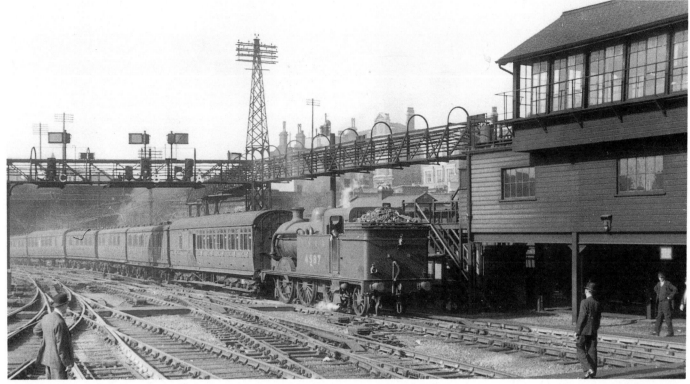

N1 class No. 4587 working a miscellany of empty coaches into King's Cross on 27th July 1935.   H. F. WHEELLER

I joined the LNER at King's Cross in 1947. I progressed through the shed preparation gang and shunting grades, learning the rudiments of firing on J52s shunting in King's Cross goods yard, Highbury Vale and Ashburton Grove. My first encounter with the N2 was on empty coach workings and passenger shunt diagrams at King's Cross terminus. They consisted of main line empty coaching stock trips to Holloway, Bounds Green and Hornsey Carriage Sidings for cleaning, and at Holloway, re-marshalling by the resident N2. In the reverse direction were the workings of main line stock, now refurbished, to King's Cross for eventual main line departure.

In spite of the N2s' comparatively small size, we had few problems in surmounting the 1 in 107 gradients of Belle Isle and Holloway. However, the Hertford North branch flyover at Wood Green, which had to be negotiated to reach Bounds Green and Hornsey carriage sidings on the up side, was more formidable. If there was any likelihood of the train being checked in Wood Green station we were held outside until the road was clear, to give us a good run at the bank.

In the vicinity of King's Cross there were many odd jobs to be performed. For example, upon the arrival of the night sleeping car train, we were called upon to pull the train clear of the platform in order to release the train engine. The coaches were then returned to the platform and the train heater turned on. Here we remained, heating the train until 8.30 am, when all passengers had to vacate their sleeping berths.

Emergencies often arose. Occasionally a main line departure train would stall inside Gas Works tunnel. We would be called upon to give the train assistance to restart on the 1 in 107 gradient. We had to proceed very cautiously into the smoke-filled tunnel, after getting the green flag from the signal box indicating 'train on line'. The guard of the stalled train was required to place three detonators on the rail immediately behind his train in such circumstances. The noise of these three detonators exploding in quick succession in the confines of the tunnel defied description. Almost immediately we would come against the buffers of the train ahead. After checking that the guard had re-joined his train, and with an exchange of

'cock-crow' whistles with the train engine, the regulator was opened and we would begin to move. The addition of the N2s' exhaust steam and smoke to the already smoke-filled tunnel was suffocating. However, eventually we reached the open at Belle Isle, only to plunge once again into the smoke of Copenhagen tunnel. The banking usually continued until Holloway box, where there was a suitable crossover to enable us to return to King's Cross station.

Another similar emergency often arose, when an ex-Moorgate train was unable to restart on the gradient out of the 'hole' (tunnel) from the Metropolitan line. On this occasion we would be coupled up to the train engine and assist as far as Finsbury Park station.

N2s were also employed on coal traffic from Highbury Vale (Finsbury Park) to High Barnet, Mill Hill and Edgware. Typical N2s in use on this working were 9546 (4767) and 9502 (4723), the latter having no condensing apparatus. The coal trains were made up at Highbury Vale, where we began our journey. The train of six or seven fully loaded 20-ton coal wagons and a guard's van, proved quite formidable

An impressive line-up of N2s awaiting rush-hour departure from King's Cross suburban platforms on 8th July 1936. Only the centre two, Nos. 4756 and 4608, can be identified. Suburban sets Nos. 56 and 57 can be seen in Platforms 15 and 17, but it was unusual to see passenger coaches in No. 17, which was generally used for milk traffic.
J. H. L. ADAMS

when climbing the 2½ miles of 1 in 59 and 1 in 63 gradients from Finsbury Park over the Northern heights. However, the N2s were usually quite adequate and there were occasions when they would 'blow off' steam with one injector working while tackling these gradients. The Highbury branch joined the LPTB electrified lines near East Finchley. At Finchley Central there were LPTB branches, over which we travelled, to reach High Barnet and Mill Hill. Beyond Mill Hill, where the LPTB line ended, we travelled over a single line to Edgware.

The coal load was mostly of the household variety but sometimes there was a load for Mill Hill gasworks. The return journey from both branches, with empties, was comparatively easy from a fireman's point of view. However, the driver's main problem, proceeding down the banks, was keeping a check on the speed of the loose-coupled wagons, with only the locomotive brake and the guard's brake to hold them back.

Eventually, I reached the 'Met' gang and the work for which Gresley originally designed the N2, the suburban passenger train services. In the 'Met' gang I joined

Three N2s waiting in No. 9 carriage road, some time in 1938.
S. FREESE

Driver Arthur Howell and we had a regular engine, 69536 (4757). We travelled many miles together, dragging the 'Quad-Arts' over the suburban routes, King's Cross to Hatfield and Welwyn Garden City and King's Cross to Hertford North, and in the reverse direction, into Broad Street, Moorgate and King's Cross.

We alternated weekly, early and late turns. On the early turn (from 2.45 am onwards – yes, AM!) we had to prepare

our engine at King's Cross top shed for the day's work. The advantage of a regular engine became obvious in its preparation. All tools, oil cans, fire irons and shovel, could be locked up and I didn't have to hunt the shed for them. Half-an-hour after signing on we left the shed for our first duty.

I remember one diagram in particular. We signed on at 2.45 am and were due to leave the shed at 3.15 am, light engine to

Gordon Hill, to make the 4.10 am into King's Cross. At that time of the morning there were several men coming off duty and with no means of transport home they headed for the 3.15 am light engine to Gordon Hill! I had to put as much coal in the firebox as I dare because once the footplate was filled with passengers, I seldom got to fire again until we reached Enfield. All I could do was sit in my seat and put the injector on now and again. There were times when it was quite an effort to get a decent fire ready for the 4.10 am departure from Gordon Hill.

I never had any trouble in supplying steam with 69536. The procedure was relatively simple. As we left a station, I turned off the injector and put several shovelfuls around the box. When the driver shut-off for the next, it was on with the injector and so on. There were a few exceptions. Sometimes we were not booked to stop at Harringay or Hornsey, when the procedure would be slightly different. In one diagram there was a real flyer – Oakleigh Park to Finsbury Park, non-stop. Travelling bunker-first and downhill all the way, it was quite a bouncy ride. Another exception was the longer distance between Gordon Hill and Cuffley. I had to be careful not to build too big a fire for the arrival at Hertford North, where we had a delay before our return working.

The driver, too, followed a regular pattern. The train was started in full forward gear (or full reverse gear if travelling up to London; it was always bunker-first to town) and usually the regulator was opened to first valve. Once the train was on the move, the driver linked up about two and a half turns of the reversing lever. When the regulator was closed for the next stop, the reversing lever was wound into full gear again. In this position the engine ran more freely while coasting.

Coming from Moorgate off the Metropolitan line and out of the 'hole' into King's Cross, up the steep gradient, presented a few problems. Although the condenser was operated inside the tunnel, we still had to hold our breath, because the atmosphere was stifling. In addition, the driver had to stop the train just in the right position at the top of the gradient, otherwise there was difficulty in restarting. As it was, the driver had to allow the train to roll backwards slightly before opening the regulator to second valve, to restart the train. This procedure could only be repeated once or twice because of catch points close behind the train. Usually we got away first time but there was the odd occasion with a spare engine when we needed assistance.

There were two types of 'Quad-Arts', gas-lit and those with electric lighting. The difference from an operating point of view was quite marked. Those with electric lighting had the additional drag from eight dynamos. If it was shed day for 69536, when she had her boiler washed out and we backed on to a train of 'Quad-Arts' with electric lighting, riding a spare engine, it wasn't a happy day!

There were two main stabling points for the 'Quad-Arts', Western Sidings on the down side of Finsbury Park, and Finsbury Park sidings on the up side. A set (7) of Pullman cars was also stabled overnight at Western Sidings, being divided into four and three cars. The 'Met' diagrams frequently began at Western or Finsbury Park Sidings. Two of the diagrams began by taking the Pullman cars from Western Sidings over the Highgate branch flyover to Finsbury Park Sidings, one engine taking four cars and the other three. This was quite an effort first thing in the morning with a comparatively cold engine.

The Gresley N2s at King's Cross were, in general, capable locomotives, although there were a few that couldn't really be called 'steam' engines. These were relegated to be spare engines. It's a great pity that only one example of that typically Gresley locomotive, the N2, remains in the shape of 4744.

No. 4749 and J52 No. 4233 awaiting their next turns on 27th July 1935. The N2 was probably about to work on one of the few through trains to Edgware. Most passengers for this destination changed at Finchley Church End into the branch service.
H. F. WHEELLER

Gresley's V1 class was an elegant design, and popular with its crews. They were all built at Doncaster, No. 416 in 1935. This was the first of the class to be provided with a hopper style of bunker, and spent its working life in the North Eastern area of the LNER.

GRESLEY SOCIETY COLLECTION

THE V1 AND V3 2–6–2Ts

ERIC NEVE

Except for brief trial periods elsewhere, all the earlier V1s were stationed at Scottish sheds. No. 2916 was at Haymarket, and is seen here in Princes Street Gardens on 4th August 1938.
L. HANSON

APART from the Beyer-Garratt No 2395, the only new tank engine class built during Sir Nigel's time as CME of the LNER was the V1 2–6–2T, later developed into the slightly more powerful V3. Outline designs were prepared for similar engines on a number of occasions, but none was proceeded with until the V1 design was finalised in 1929. The main need for this new class had arisen in Scotland, to replace N2 0–6–2T and North British 4–4–2T, and the first 34 were all allocated to sheds in the Edinburgh and Glasgow districts; more were later sent there, either from new or on transfer. Those built in 1935/36 were allocated to sheds around Newcastle, first for local services but later for the fast buffet car trains to Middlesbrough, and it was for these workings that the V3 variation was introduced in 1939. In BR days, the scope of the class in the North Eastern Region was widened to include Hull, and the coast line to Scarborough. Finally, 15 new V1s were sent to Stratford in 1938, later being seen in other parts of the GER system, but apart from brief appearances

of examples of the first batch, little was seen of them at King's Cross or Neasden.

The class appears to have been originally conceived as a tank version of the K2 2–6–0, but as the design progressed, a change was made in the boiler diameter to the (unusual for Gresley) diameter of 5ft. This was at first intended to be a suitable replacement for boilers on the NBR 'Scott' and 'Glen' 4–4–0s but was amended in several details before the first engines were built. Further, it was decided that instead of the two outside cylinders of the K2, the engines would be sufficiently large to warrant application of three-cylinder propulsion, and consequently three 16 in × 26 in cylinders were provided, the valves for the inside cylinder being operated by the usual derived gear. Boiler pressure was originally 180 lb/sq in, but raised to 200 lb in the V3, most of the original V1 being converted to the higher pressure boiler in the course of time. At first, the cab opening and bunker had a distinctive similarity to those on the N2 tanks, but on later batches the cut-away above the entrance was filled in, and a

hopper-type bunker replaced the earlier type with coal rails.

The engines were generally well received, being capable of good work when called upon, and would have been seen more widely had later orders not been cancelled. Five had been authorised in the 1940 building programme, specifically for the Southend line, and a further twenty as late as September 1941. However, wartime conditions compelled the cancellation of both these batches, in January 1943.

The second V1 ran light from Doncaster to Neasden on Tuesday, 23rd September 1930. On that day at Leicester, Driver C. Warner and Fireman P. Banyard signed on at 6.30 pm for stand-by engine and station pilot duties, and were instructed by the Running Foreman to relieve a crew working a new engine from Doncaster Works en route to London. 'Its number is 2901.' On arrival, the Doncaster crew gave the Leicester men the necessary details for working. A Works mechanic was riding through and said the engine was for Neasden Loco for later inspection at Marylebone by the CME staff, which presumably would include Gresley. After inspection, some trial runs would be made on suburban trains.

On Saturday, 27th September, I decided to take a break from observation on the GN lines and spent the afternoon in splendid isolation at Marylebone station listening to the mellow tones of GC engines and watching arrival and departure of 'Directors', 'Black Pigs' and 'Jersey Lilies', also many 4–6–2 tanks. To my intense surprise, towards the end of the afternoon, an entirely new type of engine came in to take a High Wycombe local train. No

2901 was decidedly novel to me and I was able to get a good look at it. Surprisingly, no published reports of the V1 working from Neasden have ever been seen.

Wednesday, 22nd April 1931 marked the arrival at King's Cross of V1 No 2911 for trials. It worked the 12.45 pm local to Potters Bar on the 24th and I recorded it on the 27th, but cannot remember on which train. According to R. A. H. Weight's daily logs, 2911 appeared on the 7.10 am to Cambridge on 5th, 7th and 9th May in the charge of Driver Tommy Atkins (No 2 Link), on the 4th C1 3286 was used, and on the 6th and 8th N2 2678. The 6.30 pm

to Baldock was taken on three days the following week, with Driver Nutting, and on each day of the week after that with Driver Tom Ellis. Further trips took place on both the 7.10 am and 6.30 pm trains. On Wednesday, 10th June, the V1 bade farewell to London, taking the 2.30 pm stopping train to Peterborough en route to Doncaster and eventually Ardsley, where trials were made on West Riding duties. Regrettably, no reports of these workings have been seen.

Nos. 2929 and 2909 parked at St. Margaret's shed, Edinburgh, on 1st August 1937. These would be used on suburban services to such destinations as Corstorphine and Musselburgh. L. HANSON

After Scotland's demands had been met, V1s were allocated to North Eastern sheds, for general working on Tyneside, and for the buffet car services to Middlesbrough. No. 454, of Heaton, is seen here at the Middlesbrough coaling stage in May 1937.
ERIC NEVE